Public Deficits

Perspectives in Comparative Politics

Series Editors
Professor Kay Lawson: San Francisco State University and Sorbonne, Paris.
Professor Stephen Padgett: University of Liverpool, UK.

Covering important themes in comparative politics this series is designed to bridge the gap between introductory textbooks and research literature in journals and monographs. Each book in the series surveys the theoretical literature associated with a particular topic area and then tests the theories against three country case studies.

Published titles

Cyrus Ernesto Zirakzadeh *Social Movements in Politics*

Titles in preparation

Miriam Feldblum *Immigration*
Paul A. Godt *Health Care*
Ludger Helms *Executives in Western Democracies*
Charles Olsen *Social Inequality*
Joseph Rudolph and Robert Thompson *Ethnicity*

Public Deficits:

A Comparative Study of their Economic and Political Consequences in Britain, Canada, Germany and the United States

Roland Sturm with Markus M. Müller

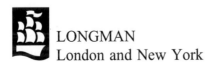

LONGMAN
London and New York

Pearson Education Limited
Edinburgh Gate
Harlow
Essex CM20 2JE
England
and Associated Companies throughout the world

Published in the United States of America
by Pearson Education Inc., New York

Visit us on the World Wide Web at:
http://www.awl-he.com

© Pearson Education Limited 1999

First published 1999

ISBN 0 582 25343 8

British Library Cataloguing-in-Publication Data
A catalogue record for this book is available from the British Library

Library of Congress Cataloging-in-Publication Data
Sturm, Roland, 1953–
    Public deficits : a comparative study of their economic and
political consequences in Britain, Canada, Germany, and the United
States / Roland Sturm.
        p.   cm. — (Perspectives in comparative politics)
    Includes bibliographical references.
    ISBN 0–582–25343–8 (ppr)
    1. Debts, Public.   2. Deficit financing.   I. Title.   II. Series.
HJ8015.S78   1999
336.3′4—dc21   98–56530
                                                                      CIP

Typeset by 35 in 10/12pt Times Roman

Printed in Malaysia, PP

Contents

Series editors' preface

Public Deficits by Roland Sturm is the second volume in a new series of books published by Pearson Education, entitled *Perspectives in Comparative Politics*. The purpose of this new series is to fill a serious gap in the literature available for the study of comparative politics by providing books that are at the same time genuinely comparative, scholarly, timely and written for a student and general readership.

The format for all these books is straightforward. Each has an introductory chapter, giving a historical and theoretical overview of the relationship between the subject in hand and the world of politics and government. This introduction is then followed by three or four case studies, in each of which the author explains the nation's constitutional-political system, gives the history of political and state involvement, and then develops the specific topics of importance as they apply to the case: the nature of the political organisations active in the domain and the tactics they employ; the external factors constraining policy; the policies presently in place; the degree of satisfaction with such policies; and probable future directions. A final chapter compares the cases, making clear the points in common, but also giving extensive recognition of the contextual differences that govern what has been accomplished, and what yet may be.

The books in this series are intended for use as advanced undergraduate, upper division or graduate level texts, as well as for a broader audience interested in the topic. They are not directed toward other specialists on the subject, but it is our hope that each will be seen as a serious and substantial work by those who know the topic best.

Such an approach requires authors (or teams of authors) deeply interested in a particular problem of politics and/or government, and well informed about the manifestation of that problem in three different nations. A great deal of effort goes into finding these authors, and we are pleased that we now have four other books under contract with authors recruited from both Europe and North America.

We are particularly pleased to include Sturm's *Public Deficits* in this exciting new series. In this volume Roland Sturm provides a remarkably clear and fully comparative explanation of a problem which assumes greater importance every day. State indebtedness has become a major issue in Western democracies. This book focuses on Britain, Canada, Germany and the United States. With their distinctive institutional and political traditions, these economic heavyweights have developed their own approach to the problem. Comparison of the four cases helps us to understand the core of the deficit problem and what it means for governments in democratic societies. This book makes it possible to understand more readily than most students and teachers would have thought possible, how public debts are acquired and managed, and the power they have to shape our lives.

Stephen Padgett and Kay Lawson

Acronyms

BEA	Budget Enforcement Act
BVerfG	Federal Constitutional Court
CBO	Congressional Budget Office
CDU	Christian Democratic Union
CEGB	Central Electricity Generating Board
CGBR	Central Government Borrowing Requirement
CHST	Canada Health and Social Transfer
CRS	Congressional Research Service
CSU	Christian Social Union
DM	German Mark
EDX	Expenditure Committee of the British Cabinet
EMU	European Monetary Union
EPF	Established Programs Financing
EU	European Union
FER	Fundamental Expenditure Review
FFB	Federal Financing Bank
GAO	General Accounting Office
GDP	Gross Domestic Product
GNP	Gross National Product
GRH	Gramm–Rudman–Hollings Act
GST	Goods and Services Tax
IMF	International Monetary Fund
IRA	Individual Retirement Account
MP	Member of Parliament
NAFTA	North American Free Trade Agreement
NCT	New Control Total
NEP	National Energy Program
NIC	National Insurance Contribution
OBRA	Omnibus Budget and Reconciliation Act
OECD	Organization for Economic Cooperation and Development
OMB	Office of Management and Budget
P & P	Priorities and Planning Committee
PAYGO	Pay-As-You-Go Rule
PEMS	Public Expenditure Management System

PES	Public Expenditure Survey
PESC	Public Expenditure Survey Committee
PLH	Provincial, Local and Hospital Sector
PPBS	Planning-Programming-Budgeting-System
PSBR	Public Sector Borrowing Requirement
RFC	Reconstruction Finance Corporation
UK	United Kingdom
USA	United States of America
ZBB	Zero-Base Budgeting

Currency exchange rates
(as of 20 January 1999)

1 US Dollar–1.6858 German Mark

1 US Dollar–0.6041 British Pound

1 US Dollar–1.5299 Canadian Dollar

Chapter 1

Introduction

Except for a brief period in Britain in the late 1980s for almost three decades now annual budget deficits have become the rule in all major industrialised countries. Public indebtedness has today reached proportions which threaten not only selected government policies, but provide a challenge to the governability of democracies. Though the belief in the long-term benevolent effects of government spending inspired by a very crude interpretation of Keynesian economic theory has been shaken fundamentally, the control of public spending has so far only made slow progress. The fairly global experience of economic crises contributes to the dilemma of mostly inflexible public spending commitments and simultaneous stagnant or shrinking tax incomes.

The inability of governments to balance their budgets is a phenomenon as old as humankind. If one compares deficits over time one finds, however, only formal continuity. Feudalism, for example, did not distinguish between public deficits and the cash needs of the monarch. Only when civil society began to free itself from the rule of the nobility, could it begin to control the budget of the state. The control of the budget emerged as the most important first right of parliaments and popular assemblies. This control was not only a check on the absolute power of the monarch, but also served to reduce the burden on the population which a monarch's spending habits used to create. Deficits were interpreted by early parliaments as a strategy of the monarchy to avoid the need for parliamentary approval of new and usually higher taxes. It is therefore not surprising that eighteenth-century economists, such as Adam Smith or David Ricardo, were extremely critical of deficits, although it is important to note that their contribution to economic theory is based on much more sophisticated arguments which have had a considerable influence on economic thought also in the nineteenth and twentieth centuries.

Populist politicians used public deficits to attack the irresponsibility of national governments. The last very successful one was Ross Perot who challenged the candidates of the Republicans and of the Democrats at the presidential elections of 1992 and 1996. What makes Perot's arguments and the arguments of his predecessors in the United States and in other countries so convincing is their commonsensical logic. The core of the arguments is that a government should not spend more than it has earned, for example, through tax income. The government budget is compared to a family budget. And everybody knows what happens to a family that is constantly in the red. It is in trouble. Firms which only borrow money and never make a profit go bankrupt. So, why should this be different with governments?

The simple answer is that when our government borrows money from our savings to finance our expenditures we owe the money borrowed to ourselves. This is not to deny that the transaction of borrowing involves costs and decisions which are not made by the citizens. But as long as borrowing only means the mobilisation of existing domestic capital for a certain price no government will go bankrupt. The ability of the government to find additional resources allows it more flexibility in budgeting, i.e. to set not only policy priorities, but also to use the wealth of a nation strategically when it believes that the time has come when spending for special public needs is justified, be it by emergency situations, the ideological aims of politicians in power, or efforts of a government to intervene in the economy and society.

If a government can act or wants to act only as a prudent head of family it will not be able to be that flexible, let alone to mobilise resources to take up a wide range of responsibilities. Economic theory which argues in favour of annually balanced budgets can therefore best be reconciled with a 'minimal state' philosophy. Not least because of the social upheaval created by the Second World War this philosophy rapidly lost influence in the post-war decades. The welfare state with its set of social policies developed. The latter were to be financed by economic growth. The role of government was to use all its resources, including borrowed money, to control economic crises and to secure full employment. Deficits accumulated in this way mattered less, not only because of the justifications for them provided by Keynesian economic thought, but also because of their still relatively small size. When interest payments on the public debt reached levels which seriously threatened the ability of governments to budget, the situation changed, however, dramatically. In the 1980s the role of the government in the economy and in society was challenged by politicians such as the British Prime Minister Margaret Thatcher or the American President Ronald Reagan. The end of big government was seen as a precondition for the end of big deficits. This conclusion implied a stronger role for policies aiming at the restructuring and the down-sizing of the welfare state and at a reordering of political priorities. In some countries, such as the United States, the deficit even became an issue in its own right. The Labor Secretary in President Clinton's first cabinet, Robert Reich (1997: 30), even spoke of 'the deficit obsession' in his country, which he assumed had deeper pyschological roots:

> The deficit has become a symbol of a government that seems out of control at the very time when large numbers of people are feeling they have less and less control over their lives. The government's failure to balance its checkbook seems particularly galling to an American public having trouble balancing its own family checkbook.

The consensus on big government and government spending was attacked and defeated in the 1980s and 1990s. The post-war assumption that the special role of the state in society and in the economy justified deficits largely disappeared. We are now back in a situation in which governments have to justify their interventions into the economy and the society and no longer their hesitation to act. As a consequence governments worldwide have developed strategies to control deficits. Some have revived the 'balanced budget' idea, others want to limit deficits by setting explicit standards for expenditure needs. The European Union in its Maastricht treaty of 1992 agreed to define sound budgetary strategies as the ones which both respect an absolute limit for the annual Public Sector Borrowing Requirement (PSBR)[1] of 3 per cent of the respective member state's GDP and a limit for the public debt total of 60 per cent of the respective member state's annual GDP. No kind of deficit control mechanism or artificially set spending limit will by itself, however, be automatically able to successfully control the development of a nation's public finances. Budgetary decisions on taxes and expenditures are always political decisions based on the distribution of power in a given society and the profit-seeking and bargaining strategies of influential interests. How these interests have worked in a historical perspective and still work today, how different countries cope with the challenge of public deficits in specific national institutional, economic, social and political circumstances, and what consequences the deficit has for the fabric of individual societies and for international relations will be the major aspects of our investigation.

One general observation with regard to the strategic choice of politicians between expenditure and taxation policies as instruments to combat the deficit can already be made here. There seems to be a general assumption that deficits are caused above all by overspending, by an unjustified largesse of governments. This is often less than half of the truth because, for example, subsidies in the form of reduced tax income (the so-called tax expenditures) may also be a very important cause for deficits. Still, in all the countries we study here, deficit reduction strategies are mostly focusing on expenditure control.

The only major exception may have been President Ronald Reagan's unsuccessful attempt during his first administration to reduce taxes in the United States in order to increase tax income. This may sound paradoxical. The idea behind this strategy was, however, that citizens who are 'overtaxed' lose the incentive to work and look for tax avoidance strategies. So tax income is much lower than it could be. In such a situation tax reductions can, indeed, raise public income, if they succeed in providing a greater motivation for the citizens to work and pay taxes. Unfortunately, it is not easy to determine in practice when we have reached the point of overtaxation. This and other practical difficulties of tax reform policies which surfaced in the context of Ronald Reagan's budget initiatives have been extensively described by his first budget director David Stockman (Stockman 1986).

For our comparison these details are not so interesting. The bottom line is, however, that at least in the countries we look at no successful national strategy exists to reduce the deficit using tax measures. And – with the exception mentioned – no strategic attempt has been made so far to develop a concept of deficit reduction policies based solely or mainly on a revision of the tax code.

Our analysis focuses on the experience of four G7 countries: Britain, Canada, Germany and the United States. These economic heavyweights with their different economic traditions, institutions and budgetary procedures have each developed their own approach to the problem of public deficits. The comparison of the four cases should help us to understand what the core of the deficit problem is and what it means for governments in democratic societies. Is the impression correct that democracies at the turn of the millennium have become obsessed with the mobilisation of resources just to stabilise the social status quo; has politics become mostly a dependent variable of budgetary needs; has the role of a politician been reduced to the job of an accountant? Or is such a perception of political realities a doomsday approach which exaggerates the financial problems democracies experience, and should we not be more optimistic and assume that the problem of public deficits is largely under control, and that with the next world-wide economic boom the spending departments of all governments will regain their ability to define first which government programmes are necessary and should have priority before they have to ask whether the financial situation allows any new programme or any redirection of expenditures at all?

Before we begin with our case studies and the comparison of the cases, it is important that we explain in greater detail what exactly we intend to investigate. So we ask, what is the public debt, and what is the theoretical background for the analysis of the deficit problem in the economic and social sciences? What in general can be assumed to be the political and social consequences of budgetary deficits, and are there any restrictions for the management of budgets in the present era of economic globalisation and economic regionalisation (European Union, North American Free Trade Agreement (NAFTA))? Answers to these questions will provide the background for the more specific analysis of the experience of Britain, Canada, Germany and the United States. To facilitate the comparison between these countries we try to elaborate on the same set of problems in each case. We look into the history of the deficit problem, we analyse the institutional framework for decisions on the deficit, we evaluate the importance of the debt problem in the national political and economic discourse, and we investigate the effects of deficit control policies. The concluding chapter of this book focuses on an in-depth comparison of the four cases analysed and ventures to put the problem of public deficits into a political science perspective. As we will see there is considerable evidence that Britain, Canada and the United States are about to succeed with their efforts to control their deficits and possibly also the growth of their public debt, whereas for Germany it seems that only dark clouds are on the horizon.

To make the case studies more accessible it may be helpful to keep in mind that our cases are three parliamentary political systems (Britain, Canada and Germany) and one presidential political system. Why is this important for budgetary decision-making? First of all it means that we can expect decision-making processes to be more similar in Britain, Canada and Germany than in the United States. In the United States we find a clear division of powers which has been confirmed by the Supreme Court also with regard to specific details such as the 'Gramm–Rudman–Hollings Act' and the 'line-item veto' (for details see Chapter 5 on the United States). Congress decides on the budget. It has the 'power of the purse'. In parliamentary democracies the formal decision on the budget is also made by parliament. But, because the executive is elected by the parliamentary majority which, of course, supports the government it has elected, the 'power of the purse' has in practice been handed over to the government of the day. Why can governments in parliamentary democracies expect that given normal circumstances its support by a parliamentary majority will be stable?

This can be explained by a second difference between parliamentary political systems and the presidential system of the United States. Political parties in parliamentary democracies are held together by a strong sense of party discipline which originally was based on a common ideology. Voting against the government's budget would probably either mean for the single representative to lose her or his parliamentary party membership or – if a greater number of representatives were to vote against the government – this would be the end of this government. If the President in the United States, however, is losing a vote in Congress on a budgetary plan he supports, there is no need for him to retire.

This brings us to a third difference between parliamentary and presidential political systems. The President in the United States has his own mandate. He is elected in general elections and is in this respect not dependent on parliamentary majorities. It is therefore not surprising that whereas in parliamentary democracies we find a process of joint decision-making on budgets, which includes both the Executive and Parliament, in the United States budgets can be developed separately both by the President and by Congress. Though, as already said, Congress decides, the President is not involved in the decision-making process via party political channels in the disciplined way this is the case for a government in parliamentary democracies where the executive is almost the only powerful decision-maker. Whereas in parliamentary decision-making processes the budget which gets its final approval by parliament has the consent of the government of the day, an American President may still veto the budget acts Congress has agreed on.

What is the public debt?

It is difficult to understand the concrete meaning of abstract debt totals which sum up the national debt accumulated in a given country. No citizen has ever seen or will ever see the pile of banknotes equivalent to several billions or trillions of public debt in a given currency. Economists tell us that what counts are not abstract numbers, but the relationship of the accumulated debt to the economic strength of a national economy over time and the way a deficit is financed. With regard to the latter the important question is, whether a deficit is financed by state borrowing from abroad, as has often been the case in Third World countries, or whether the deficit can be financed at home through the mobilisation of private savings, in other words the willingness of citizens to lend their money to the state in return for income created by the interest rates the state pays. Whereas deficit financing by state borrowing, for example from the International Monetary Fund, creates political dependency and implies the acceptance of conditions for a country's economic and social policies, borrowing from the national and international capital markets has no such implications for national sovereignty.

Still, there is a lively debate centering on the question 'when is the public debt too big and becomes a danger for the functioning of a national economy?'. To answer such a question one needs to agree on indicators which may measure the quality of the public debt with regard to a country's economic performance, and/or which allow an international comparison which evaluates the size of the accumulated debt. Journalists like to use the ratio of indebtedness per person as a very illuminating indicator, because then they can argue, for example, how many thousand dollars or German marks every citizen in theory has to pay to make up for the amount of money the public sector has already borrowed. This indicator is misleading not only because it uses a hypothetical scenario, but also because it connects economic problems with demographic change. To keep the public debt at its present level this indicator would demand a birth rate which increases at the same rate as inflation. No one would seriously believe that a higher birth rate, which in case it increases faster than inflation, numerically reduces the 'personal debt', would automatically change the economic situation of a country for the better.

The best indicators for the size of the debt problem are those which are directly connected to a country's economic performance, for example, the debt-to-GDP ratio. This indicator was used, as mentioned, to define the debt limit for the Maastricht criteria. Two other indicators for the importance of the debt problem are also useful, because they hint at the consequences of the public debt. They focus on the interests to be paid annually for the public debt. Interest rates per se do not tell us much about public borrowing when we compare the four countries which interest us here. In all four countries interest rates are fairly similar due to their relative stable economic performance and their importance for the world financial markets. If we were to discuss Italy or Greece as well, not to mention Hungary, or Russia or other non-member states of the OECD, interest rates could tell us something about the relative importance of the national debt problem. For our comparison we need to look at interest rates in perspective. One indicator, the ratio of interests to tax income, shows how much of the national income raised is simply needed to service the national debt, and a second, the ratio of interests to public expenditures, indicates how strongly the decision-making on the annual budget suffers from restrictions caused by the debt burden. To improve on the relevance of figures for the public debt it is not very helpful, however, if state debts are compared with state assets. Whereas this is a useful figure in business accounting – for businesses may sell their assets when going bankrupt – it is obviously meaningless for the assessment of government financial policies. States cannot go bankrupt, and they can only sell their assets up to certain limits.

We have so far assumed that we all know what the state is and that we are therefore able to calculate the debt total. What sounds easy in theory can create enormous difficulties in practice. One reason for the misunderstandings and mistakes made in comparing public debt across nations is the fact that on the national level several definitions of the public sector may co-exist, and that for the sake of comparison different concepts are used (Lane 1993: 12ff.). A brief look at the degree of centralisation of taxes and expenditures may suffice to illustrate that conclusions drawn only from the comparison of national budgets and national debt

Table 1.1 Degree of centralisation (share of the national level in %) of taxes and expenditures (1983)

	Taxes	Expenditures
Britain	83.9	89.2
Canada	46.4 (1982)	52.4 (1982)
Germany	48.0	43.3
USA	57.4	58.2

Source: Sturm 1989: 121f.

totals are grossly misleading. In federal countries the financial situation of sub-national governments is in our context of utmost importance.

For the calculation of debt totals there is also the question of inclusion or exclusion of the debt burden of social security funds and off-budget funds. The budgets of the social security systems in the United States and in Germany, for example, are institutionally separated from government budgets. Off-budget funds have grown in importance in many countries, because we have witnessed a flight out of the budget mainly in order to create a more positive impression of the debt problem which is actually more severe (Gantner 1994). 'Creative budgeting' of this kind which uses legal niceties to 'massage' a budget in order to meet certain criteria, such as the ones for membership in the European Monetary Union (EMU) or deficit targets set by Congressional legislation in the United States, may have the political effects hoped for. But it is extremely doubtful whether international and national monetary markets can be deceived so easily.

Off-budget public deficits have mushroomed in some countries. In Germany, especially after unification and with the privatisation of state monopolies, for example the railways, money had to be borrowed from capital markets for special purposes. The deficits and interest payments which were the logical consequence come from off-budget funds. This strategy formally avoided some of the increase of the federal deficit. Off-budget funds are not unique to Germany. In the United States, the Federal Financing Bank (FFB) was used as a device to manipulate the public deficit. It shouldered the deficit of a number of government agencies. Formally, this eliminated their deficits. As the deficit total of the FFB was not included into the calculations of the federal deficit totals (Wildavsky 1988: 125ff.; Bickley 1985), the public deficit seemed to be lower than it actually was. Another American example is the handling of the Savings and Loans crisis following the bankruptcy of the Federal Savings and Loans Insurance Company in the late 1980s. To meet the deficit targets set by the Gramm–Rudman–Hollings legislation in Congress only the interest rates paid by the federal government for the deficit, which were needed to meet the costs of the bankruptcy, were included into the annual budget, not, however, the deficit itself (OECD 1990: 79ff.).

In the public debate the short-term interest focuses on the annual deficit which, of course, contributes to the debt total. This is worth mentioning, because a reduction of annual borrowing (compared to the previous financial year) is often misunderstood as a reduction of the public debt, which it is not. New borrowing may it be smaller or bigger than last year's, always contributes to the debt total and increases the proportion of expenditures needed to cover the interest rates to be paid on the public debt, if interest rates remain stable or rise.

For Britain, as the only non-federal country in our comparison, it is much easier to control the annual deficit of all levels of government than it is for federal states. Britain therefore watches closely the development of the annual Public Sector Borrowing Requirement which is taken to be an indicator for the development of the public debt. The PSBR is the annual fiscal deficit, i.e. the total borrowings of the public sector – central government, local government and public corporations combined. It measures the difference between public spending and taxation. As the former Treasury 'mandarin' Leo Pliatzky (1982: 192) has pointed out, the PSBR is an instrument of budgetary control:

> The PSBR is a creation of the Treasury's – the concept is not used at all in France or the United States, for instance – and it is what the Treasury say it is, i.e. borrowing by public sector bodies. It is who does the borrowing that counts, not where the borrowing comes from . . . [The PSBR] consists of the central government borrowing requirement (the CGBR) plus the market and overseas borrowing of nationalised industries, plus the market and overseas borrowing of the local authorities.

The problem with PSBR is that, at least as long as nationalised industries do still play a role in the national economy, it adds up two kinds of deficits of different nature and purpose (the firm and the state). In federal states the debate on the deficit focuses most of the time on the deficit at the national level. Only the Maastricht criteria have recently forced German decision-makers to pay greater attention to the overall annual deficit of all levels of government.

With regard to the annual deficit, similar to the definitions of public debt, it is possible to develop indicators which measure its relative size. One possibility is to look at the ratio of annual borrowing and the GDP, the indicator used, for example, by the European Union's Maastricht criteria. Another indicator which may facilitate the interpretation of deficits is the ratio of the annual deficit to annual expenditures. This indicator illustrates the extent to which expenditures are credit-financed. To know more about the causes of the deficit it may also be helpful to distinguish between primary and secondary causes for the deficit. The primary deficit would consist of the short-fall of revenues for financing expenditures, the secondary deficit would also include the costs of the public debt, i.e. the amount of money needed to pay for the interests on the public debt (Schlesinger *et al.* 1993: 23).

The evolution of the deficit

If we want to understand the growth of deficit over time in different countries a theoretical framework would be useful which allows generalisations. The historical and circumstantial explanations of the growth of deficits we can find are, however, often not very sophisticated. Still, some of these explanations are ambitious and try at least to develop some systematic insights. The already mentioned Scottish eighteenth-century philosopher and economist Adam Smith in his classical *Inquiry into the Nature and Causes of the Wealth of Nations* (1776) has described a situation which in his view inevitably leads to public deficits, namely war. He argues that the amount of money needed for a war over a short time cannot be raised overnight, not even if taxes are increased. So governments in war times have to rely on deficits.

Another classical contribution to the explanation of the growth of public expenditures can be found in the work by Adolph Wagner, a German economist who published in the late nineteenth and early twentieth century. Wagner observed that in the nineteenth century the state began to expand its activities both quantitatively and qualitatively. In addition to its traditional tasks, such as its role in war and peace or in the provision of law and order, it took on new responsibilities, for example with regard to the development of infrastructures (e.g. the building of railway lines), the provision of health services or the support of industrialisation. Wagner assumed that this was not accidental, but constituted a statistical trend, which he put into a formula later called Wagner's law (Wagner 1911: 734). Wagner's law expects a permanent growth of public expenditures parallel to the evolution of the cultural and economic wealth of a country. If this was indeed 'a law', it is hard to see how the tax income of the state could keep up with expenditure needs. A growing public debt would be the inevitable consequence.

The weakness of Wagner's conclusions, which he derived from his analysis of nineteenth-century statistical trends is, however, obvious. What he provides is a description contingent on historical circumstances, not a theoretical concept. It has also been mentioned that his 'Law' is not testable. Still, he found an echo in science, and a number of authors have tried to identify historical circumstances which contribute to expenditure growth. There seems to be a consensus with regard to the fact that the two World Wars were not only responsible for a temporary rise in expenditures, as Adam Smith would have argued, but also for a general increase in the level of public expenditure in the post-war years (Kohl 1985: 36ff.). This does certainly not imply the automatic consequence of deficits, but it explains at least some of the difficulties countries had in the post-war years with balancing their budgets.

Marxists have tried to identify the context of economic developments which lead to deficits and which challenge the uneasy social coalition the welfare state in their view is based upon. They argue that on the one hand there are the demands on the resources of the state by industry, by a coalition of capitalists who profit from defence expenditures and by the general public which is kept loyal to capitalism by a wide range of social policies. On the other hand there is, they argue, the reality of governments unable to raise public income fast enough to provide for these resources. The conflict which arises from this structural defect of capitalism leads the state into a fiscal crisis (O'Connor 1973). The substance of the crisis is embodied in the fact that every strategy the state chooses to break out of its financial impasse, for example by increasing taxes, reduces its legitimacy (and so was the hope of Marxists will bring nearer the end of capitalism). In the Marxist analysis the state cannot attack the interests of the capital-owners, because they control the state. If the state attacks welfare spending, this causes a massive wave of protests and increases the risk of more militant social unrest. So the only choice that remains for governments is either higher deficits or the acceptance of a new equilibrium of social forces. This new equilibrium may mean the end of the welfare state dictated by a rightist government in spite of all social resistance or, alternatively, the end of capitalism.

The major problem with this analysis is that the choices it offers are very much influenced by a special brand of crisis theory which sees in every problem of capitalist development the first sign of an imminent breakdown of capitalism. We have witnessed in all major industrialised countries a paradigmatic change which transformed the welfare state in the 1980s and 1990s, but the revolution Marxists expected did not occur. What their view offers is again above all a description and interpretation of social change which may lead to deficits.

In spite of efforts, such as the ones described in this chapter, to develop a more systematic approach to the explanation of the historical development of deficits our knowledge of general rules for the evolution of the deficit is limited. Probably no one would dispute the fact that an increase of public expenditures (whatever explanation or justification one may find for it) can cause financial problems for public budgets. But no convincing argument has been made so far which explains why tax income automatically has to fall behind public expenditures (one potential source of the deficit problem) or why the historical level of public expenditures is inflexible and cannot be reduced if necessary (another potential source of the deficit problem). Our four country studies will demonstrate that public debt is much more the result of specific historical, political and institutional circumstances than of general trends or 'iron laws'.

Public deficits in the light of economic theories

Economic advice on the deficit

Economists have dealt less with the question of how social change may explain the development of deficits. They accept that deficits are an *economic* phenomenon for which an *economic* explanation can be found. The economic analysis of the deficit usually has as its frame of reference a more general economic theory. In other words, when economists engage in controversies on the deficit this reflects their differences of approach with regard to the analysis of reality, or, simply put, their respective preferences for one or the other (often mathematical) economic model. Though models are a scientific tool, one should not make the mistake of easily dismissing their importance for practical politics. The theoretical contributions of economists serve as powerful weapons to legitimise political decisions, even if decision-makers do not always bother to understand their complexity.

This can be illustrated by the influence of a simple chain of arguments successfully introduced by the Chairman of the US Federal Reserve, Alan Greenspan, into the decision-making process of the Clinton administration. Greenspan argued (Reich 1997: 64f.):

Unless the federal government makes a radical commitment to balancing the budget, global lenders (including Americans themselves) will demand higher and higher interest payments on loans to businesses in the United States because the demand for private savings will far outstrip the supply. Private investment will thus decline. As a result, productivity will slow and inflation will accelerate.

This argument relates the deficit to reduced economic productivity and the danger of inflation. But is there any empirical evidence for this scenario which frightens, of course, every politician? The answer is no. There is no economic law which determines a direct relationship between deficits and interest rates, for example, and it is a mere assumption that private investors in a situation of global markets will not be able to find cheap investment capital. Other economists see the relationship between deficits and interest rates quite differently. James Tobin (1984: 11) argues, for example, that 'the deficit is mostly a result, not cause, of recent and current high interest rates and the depression caused by those rates'. Thus, for him the cure for economic ills is obvious: the national bank shall expand credit by reducing interest rates in order to stimulate an economic recovery, which will in turn increase tax revenues and eventually reduce the deficit. In such controversies details do not count, what counts is the political impact of these and other economic theories which explain the deficit and look into its economic consequences. In every political era one can identify economic theories who found general acceptance in a society and influenced consciously or unconsciously political decision-makers.

In the rest of this chapter we intend to look with a critical eye on the most important economic explanations for the deficit and the most important advice given by economists on how politicians should deal with the deficit. The so-called 'classical school' of economics from which Alan Greenspan took his arguments would stress, as mentioned above, the negative effects of deficits for the economy. It would argue that deficits hurt the economy. Budget deficits are expected to 'crowd out' private investment, since public bodies, e.g. the government, compete for the same financial resources on the capital markets as private investors. The government's demand pushes up interest rates. An increase in interest rates is a negative incentive for investors. They are likely to down-size their planned investments. This hurts both economic growth and employment. As a further consequence high interest rates attract foreign capital. This puts pressure on the national currency. The financial markets will tend to favour an upward revaluation. Such a revaluation of the national currency damages a country's export industries, since its products now become more expensive on foreign markets.

Policy-makers should therefore, it is argued, reduce the need for deficit-financed expenditures, thus reducing the pressure on the capital markets. Such a strategy could create new investments, new jobs and even additional tax income which would make it easier to balance the budget. One critical variable for the validity of this model is time. When, if the model is correct, can we expect these positive consequences, and are they available in all circumstances? A second critical variable is the distribution of benefits and losses when the government decides to reduce its expenditure programmes (a move which is often accompanied by the costly creation of incentives for investments). How does society react to attacks on the welfare state? An answer to these two sets of questions could be that a government which follows the advice of the 'classical school' of economics would have to accept for its economic policies (and in most countries exactly this is the case today) that preference has to be given to the success of industry. It would also have to reduce mass incomes and social welfare.

This, as it is called, strengthening of the 'supply-side' of the economy, i.e. the reduction of costs and regulations for industry, does neither guarantee reduced deficits, let alone at a reduction or elimination of deficits at a certain point in time, which the government choses, nor is it a plausible choice in the eyes of those citizens affected by expenditure cuts. The classical school of economics only has the negative advice for the government to do less. Governments who take this advice have to believe that sooner or later economic success will be produced by market forces, and that economic success will create enough tax income to balance their budgets. Ironically to some extent the classical school of economics may claim success with regard to the control of deficits even if an economy remains weak. If a government can reduce its expenditures to the levels of its tax income, no matter how small this is, the deficit disappears in a less successful economy, too.

In contrast to the classical school of economics which dominated the economic argument till the early twentieth century and has experienced a revival during the last two decades, the contribution of John Maynard Keynes to economic theory defined an active role for governments in the economy. He saw deficits more positively as a strategic instrument for policy-makers in times of crises.

The most important difference between a Keynesian view of economics and that of the classical school concerns the role of the state in the economy. Political interventions into the economy are no longer regarded as disruptive, but as a contribution to economic stability. The task of the government, when there is unemployment, is to borrow and to spend in order to make up at least temporarily for the lack of private demand. The purposes for which the government spends money in an economic crisis are less important in Keynes's view than the government activity itself. When there is unemployment 'wasteful loan expenditure may nevertheless enrich the community on balance. Pyramid building, earthquakes, even wars may serve to increase wealth.' These are Keynes's famous examples mentioned in Chapter 10 of his *General Theory of Employment, Interest, and Money* first published in 1936. In essence, Keynes encourages governments to spend their way out of an economic crisis no matter whether this causes deficits, and irrespective of other deliberations. Some of his disciples even went further. Abba P. Lerner, for instance, has argued that in periods of unemployment, government spending, no matter whether it is financed through borrowing or even the printing of money, is automatically beneficial. He even comes to the conclusion (Lerner 1983: 48):

> This means that the absolute size of the national debt does not matter at all, and that however large the interest payments that have to be made, these do not constitute any burden upon society as a whole.

Certainly only a few economists and an even smaller group of politicians would today share these radical views. But one does not need to wait for the arguments of the critics of Keynesianism to evaluate this economic theory. The real test for Keynesianism was its practical application in western democracies during the post-war decades. Today we know that Keynesianism unfortunately did not have the undisputed recipe for a successful management of economic crises. It left behind a growing burden of public debt in all industrialised countries.

So the question is what went wrong? If we ignore for a moment the fact that national models for steering the economy are always difficult to implement in an era in which economies rapidly internationalise, three factors may explain the failure of post-war Keynesianism:

(a) the disjunction of business cycles and electoral cycles, or, to put it more bluntly, the fact that in pre-election periods politicians were unwilling to use government income for repaying deficits incurred during times of crises. There were votes for additional expenditures, but no votes for fiscal rectitude. And as a result the accumulated debt was kept and every new economic crisis added to it.

(b) the social dimension of the welfare state. This meant an expansion of expenditures for the disadvantaged and the provision of more public goods and services. The temptation for politicians to use the economic argument in favour of deficits to justify such policies was great. Even in times of crisis the distinction between spending on consumption and spending on investments became blurred. To finance the welfare state by deficit-spending had another big political advantage. It avoided distributional conflict. If the poorer social strata were given the same amount of goods and services they received without deficit-spending, the financial means for these transfers would have had to come out of the pocket of the richer strata. Instead of distributing goods and services the state would have had to redistribute them from one social group to the other. This would not have been possible without political conflict. Deficit-spending Keynesian style avoided such social and political conflict.

(c) Keynesianism provided a tool for coping with the cyclical crises of the business cycle. After the oil shock of 1973–4 all major economies were, however, also afflicted by structural crises, i.e. the lack of competitiveness of their national economies. To overcome these crises structural changes in the national economies were needed which could not be brought about by budgetary policies alone. The major changes needed were to be made on the level of the individual company. It took political decision-makers too long to recognise this new problem. As a result deficit-spending was used in an inefficient way. The structural problems of national economies could not be overcome by state-financed investment programmes. Though these were inefficient, their costs accelerated the growth of the public debt.

The fact that deficits had become an integral part of national economic strategies in the post-war decades led economists to assume that they constituted a regular feature of government budgets. Those who wanted to argue that this feature was not going to create economic problems could refer to the work of the economist Evsey

D. Domar (1944). Domar had argued that as long as the growth rate of the public debt in the long run equals the economic growth rate of an economy, a growing debt burden will have no negative effects on an economy. This means, of course, that you need to be an optimist if you do not want to get worried. Who guarantees economic growth, and what should be done with the public debt in times of economic crises?

In Germany the Council of Economic Advisors (*Sachverständigenrat zur Begutachtung der gesamtwirtschaftlichen Entwicklung*) used a similar notion. They tried to define an annual deficit which had no effects on the business cycle. This 'neutral' annual deficit was supposed to consist mainly of the deficit of a size the German public opinion had become 'used to' (de facto an average of earlier deficits) modified by tax shortfalls or greater tax income due to the economic situation or inflation. The assumption that one can calculate a quasi-normal deficit allowed the Council to argue that actual deficits were either too small (!) or too big. In the spirit of Keynesianism, the Council allowed, however, a deviation from the deficit, i.e. a reduction of the deficit to counteract inflationary tendencies in the economy and an increase of the deficit to stimulate the economy in times of crises (Barth 1981).

Approaches such as Domar's or one of the German Council of Economic Advisors have been critisised for creating the impression that policy-makers could live happily with the public debt. Their affirmative view together with the popularity of Keynesianism were made responsible for the dire financial straits many industrialised countries are in today. Justifications for overspending and deficits do not explain, of course, decisions of governments. From the point of view of politicians it was certainly convenient to refer to accepted economic theories which they may not have understood in every detail, but which served their purposes very well, because they provided legitimacy for a political course they wanted to follow anyhow. Today Keynesians would argue that the reduction of their policy advice to the simple idea of government spending in times of crisis does not do justice to their ideas. They have also learnt from past policy failures and would argue that in the last two decades the differences between them and the classical school of economics were exaggerated.

Explaining the deficit

Of less importance for political decision-making are efforts by economists to explain why there are deficits and what the reasons are for differences in the size of deficits between countries. These explanations try to go beyond the obvious fact that deficits are the result of a mismatch of public income and public expenditures. Economists are also not content to explain this mismatch by the economic fortunes of different countries. Their hypothesis is that at the root of the deficit problem lie individual decisions which are translated into politics. This process does not automatically guarantee a true picture of the individual preferences of citizens. They can be distorted by a wide range of institutional arrangements (party politics, parliament, the role of the finance minister to name just a few) which intervene between preferences and policy outcomes. Deficits in the perspective of that kind of analysis are the result of public choice (the theories we deal with here are therefore known as public choice theories) under institutional restrictions. The task of economists who work in the framework of the public choice theory is to come up with mathematical models which explain and predict actual policy outcomes as exactly as possible.

What this means can be better understood by looking at what economists identified as the given preferences of individuals. From the point of view of the individual it may seem rational to demand as much as possible from the state. It has been pointed out that it is rather the lack of information of the individual with regard to his or her needs and of the possible personal benefits of certain expenditures than any other factor which restricts individual demands. As there is never full information of that kind for all individuals, government budgets, according to Downs (1959–60), tend to be 'too small'. This is, of course, just a hypothesis which depends critically on the definition of full information.

It is certainly true, however, that citizens have a preference for government expenditures over taxation. The individual as taxpayer is very reluctant to contribute to the state's income, whereas expenditures, especially when they benefit large special interest groups (of old-age pensioners, car-owners, etc.), are easily accepted. Taxes, which in most cases are not dedicated to special purposes, are seen as a burden for goods and services which the state would provide even if one individual would not pay for them. Many of the goods provided by the state are public goods (defence, infrastructure), i.e. goods which social interaction, especially the market process, does not automatically produce, but which citizens want.

The problem is that the value of any particular expenditure to the individual recipient seems greater than its cost to the individual as taxpayer. Benefits from expenditures are immediate and tangible, taxation seems to be a contribution to a non-transparent fund controlled by others. So, if only individual preferences were the yardstick, the result would probably be a shrinking tax base confronted with expenditures growth, i.e. in other words permanent deficits and an ever-growing national debt. Economists have argued that this logic has some importance for practical politics. The 'rational' behaviour of politicians and citizens is said to result regularly in a financial disaster, because voters do not understand the budgetary constraints of governments and politicians tend to profit from their 'fiscal illusion' by getting away with increased spending without presenting the bill to the electorate in the form of higher taxes (Buchanan and Wagner 1977). In the words of Alesina and Perotti (1995: 9):

> When offered a deficit-financed expenditure program, they (the voters, the authors) overestimate the benefits of current expenditures and underestimate the future tax burden. Opportunistic politicians who want to be re-elected take advantage of this confusion by raising spending more than taxes in order to please the 'fiscally illuded' voters.

Some theories of democracy which expect the state to perform the function of a guardian of the common good would regard it as one of the state's foremost tasks to put up a barrier against the growth of public debt caused by individual demands. But there are also other theories of democracy, especially those who follow the ideas of Joseph Schumpeter (1942), who define the role of politicians differently. For them politicians are above all political entrepreneurs who need to listen carefully to what citizens want and have to react to popular demands in order to get elected. In the Schumpeterian world the common good is not predetermined by or even known to governments, but is the by-product of a power struggle of competing party elites. Even if politicians do not have to rely on campaign contributions they may bid up voters' expectations and commit themselves to certain spending programmes during the election campaign. They find it, however, more difficult to raise taxes and to reduce spending as long as a potential majority of the voters does not have these preferences.[2]

Early public choice theories had to rely on these general assumptions if they wanted to explain deficits. More recent theoretical efforts have tried to include as many specific institutional arrangements as possible in order to shed light on the institutional restrictions for the translation of individual preferences into policies, such as electoral laws, party systems, budget laws, the role of central banks, divided government in the case of the United States, coalition government or the degree of (de)centralisation of political decision-making (federalism).

So far, economic modelling is, however, not sophisticated enough to cope with the complexities of budgetary developments in different societies. Though efforts have been made to look for models which integrate a broader range of causal explanations for public deficits and the growth of the public debt these have not succeeded yet in constructing a model with sufficient explanatory power. Explanations offered often do not exceed in their quality common-sense assumptions (Wagschal 1996). If one wants to know more about the public debt, it is therefore advisable to focus, as we will do here, at least as a first step on case studies, for which adequate and reliable information on the context of decisions on deficits can be provided.

Political and social consequences of public deficits

We can be more specific with regard to the political and social consequences of deficits. The major effect of a growing debt burden certainly is that an ever-growing part of the annual budget has to be used to finance interests on the debt. This has at least two consequences: one is that an ever-larger part of the budget becomes hostage to unpredictable swings in interest rates and more importantly that the power of decision-making of governments of the day is severely reduced. If one takes into account that in addition to the amount of money which has to be set aside to pay for interests on debt there is a huge share of the expenditure total which are entitlements, expenditures to which individual citizens are entitled by law, it is quite clear that there remain precious few financial means for governments to actively pursue their new policies. At the extreme end of such a process government is reduced to administering financial gridlock.

The financing of investments by public debt has been justified as burden-sharing between generations. The argument was made that investments today profit not only the present, but also future generations. Newman (1968: 193) has argued:

> Some government programs are of a very long-range nature, and their immediate benefits may be of little import. For example, an elaborate hydroelectric project involving the construction of a large dam across a major stream may take a number of years to complete. To expect things of this sort to be financed entirely by current taxes during the actual period of construction is perhaps asking too much of a taxpayer's sense of responsibility toward future generations. Without borrowing, such projects may never be undertaken, no matter how desirable in terms of long-range community welfare.

It was therefore seen as only just if these generations contribute during a later time period by repaying the debts incurred today. This is Richard Musgrave's (1959: 558ff.) 'pay as you use' argument. The future users of investments pay for them while they profit from them. Whether this is a correct notion of intergenerational justice can be debated. One problem seems to be the lack of voice of future generations with regard to the nature of investment decisions. Who can be sure that one of the future generations would have opted for nuclear energy, for example, when nuclear waste will now be around costing money for thousands of years? Another problem lies in the lack of guarantees for the success of debt-financed investments. If they fail, future generations still have to shoulder the financial burden though it would hardly be just to blame them for mistakes made one or two generations earlier. The alternative would obviously be to save before you use and to avoid new debts.

A very popular fear with regard to the effects of public deficits is that government borrowing absorbs private-sector savings that could otherwise finance private investments. We have already identified this argument as one of the central ones of the classical school of economics. The crowding-out model suffers from the implicit assumption of a closed national capital market. In today's international capital markets it is highly unlikely that states are able to efficiently crowd out private investments, just as it is unlikely that interest rates can be set only with regard to national economic conditions. It is possible that private investments could be sustained by private foreign borrowing, which, of course, has a price. Such borrowing would produce increased foreign indebtedness and increased interest and dividend payments abroad. Economists cannot agree on the real effects of crowding out and empirical studies are inconclusive. However, there is at least a psychological dimension to the problem. German bankers, including the *Bundesbank* board members, are sure that over time the flow of investments is unfavourably affected by public sector deficits (Schlesinger *et al.* 1993: 148ff.).

Another psychological consequence of the unrestricted growth of the public debt may be higher inflation. Inflationary expectations are created by the belief that persistent deficits will drive up interest rates and jeopardise economic stability. A weak economy with a growing money supply because of extensive public borrowing looks like a role model for permanent inflation. This impression may adversely affect consumer and investor confidence and may thus dampen spending and investment. Exact proof for this assumption remains, however, difficult too (Doern, Maslove and Prince 1988: 26).

But there may also be some positive effects of the deficit for some groups of society. Very often capital owners are expected to be the ones who benefit from deficits. They are said to profit from the relatively high interest rates the state has to pay in order to borrow money. There have been doubts, however, whether the mechanics of borrowing, as explained by the so-called 'transfer approach', are really redistributive in their effects. The transfer approach argues that government bonds are usually sold to social groups with relatively high income. These groups thus receive the largest part of interest payments on the government debt. Taxes on the other hand, including the taxes needed to pay the interests on the national debt, have to be paid by everybody, including the poorer social groups. This means that the well-to-do, who hold government bonds, do not pay (via taxes) their full share of interests on the national debt, since they receive interest payments. Or to put it more bluntly, the rest of the population helps to finance interests which are income for the rich.

In 1968 the *Wissenschaftliche Beirat beim Bundeswirtschaftsministerium* (Advisory Group to the German Economics Minister) asked for a more detailed analysis of this problem. The literature which took up this challenge rejected the transfer approach. It argued that there is no logical link between taxes (even those that finance the debt interests) and the income which private capital investors derive from interests. The fact that capital investors bought government bonds is irrelevant in this context. They could have just as well bought any other bond or stocks. Receiving interest payments has nothing to do with the size of the national debt, but only with the fact that capital investors had capital to buy bonds. The relative distribution of government bonds is thus of no concern for the distribution of debt costs for individuals.

Debt management policies

The size and the development of the public debt can be influenced by policies which 'manage' both debt repayment and the strategies for borrowing money on the capital markets. The higher interest rates are, for example, which have to be paid on borrowed money, the faster will be the growth of the public debt total. New debts have to be funded regularly by the markets in order to get the necessary funds to pay off old debts which come due. This mechanism is called 'debt refunding'.

To understand government activities in the field of debt management it is important to get familiar with some more technical details. A basic fact is: in the case of borrowing money from someone, or lending money to someone respectively, there has to be some agreement on the conditions for the repayment of the capital and the interest rates to be paid. This form of legal representation of the right to receive prospective future benefits under stated conditions is usually referred to as 'security' (Sharpe and Alexander 1990: 3). Securities may be issued either by private corporations or by public bodies. A 'bond' represents a fairly long-term commitment on the part of the issuer (the borrower) to the investor (the lender). This commitment is to make cash payments each year (the coupon amount) up to some point in time (the maturity date), when a single final cash payment (the principal) will also be made. The amount for which such bonds can be bought and sold varies from time to time. While coupon payments may be easily predicted, the end-of-period selling price of a security is quite uncertain at the beginning of the relevant period, which makes it difficult to predict the expected return, if the (original) investor is going to sell it before maturity.

Everything said so far holds for both corporate and public securities. There are, however, also a couple of important differences between them. Public loans carry little risk. It is certain that payments will be made as promised. Moreover, the rate of return is known, at least at the beginning of any single period. It may vary, however, quite significantly from one period to another. For example, the return on one form of public securities in the United States, known as Treasury Bills, ranged from a high of 14.71 per cent per year in 1981 to a low of virtually zero in 1940, with an average value of 3.51 per cent during the 1926–86 period (Ibbolson and Sinquefield 1983: 7–12; Sharpe and Alexander 1990: 6). Treasury Bills represent a loan to the Treasury Department on a short-term basis. This form of security exists in all countries. In the United States these securities are sold at a discount with maturities of up to 52 weeks in denominations of $10.000 or more. US Treasury Bills are brought to the market by auction, however, there is also a secondary market since those papers are marketable.

Another form of government securities are Saving Bonds. These are also long-term securities, but in contrast to others Saving Bonds are non-marketable papers which are sold to individuals and special organisations only (Sharpe/Alexander 1990: 325–31). Over two-thirds of the public debt in the United States, for instance, is marketable, i.e. can be sold at any time by the original purchaser through government securities dealers. Saving Bonds do exist in Germany, for example, too. They offer some advantages to their holders in comparison to other government bonds. The restrictions attached to Saving Bonds are intended to have the effect of influencing the overall composition of the group of investors who hold government securities. With the special conditions under which Saving Bonds operate governments want to win over the pro-verbal man in the street as investor. In the United States the federal government itself is a large holder of government bonds, as is the Federal Reserve System. A large amount is also held by state and local governments as well as private investors of one sort or another. These securities are, for example, a major asset of the portfolios of commercial banks and other financial institutions.

Four debt management goals can be identified (Pampel 1993: 10): (1) fiscal goals. This means that the government aims at the lowest possible costs for financing its debt; (2) allocation goals, i.e. public borrowers attempt to find strategies for borrowing money from private and corporate investors which have only the smallest possible influence on the development of interest rates. It is also intended that debt refunding should cause no major cost increases for governments, i.e. maturity dates in times of high interest rates should be avoided; (3) distributive goals. This means that the social composition of all creditors of the state shall reflect criteria of social justice, at least to some extent. For instance, governments try to involve lower income earners as creditors, who would otherwise only be able to save money in low-interest saving accounts. If they invest in securities, they will also enjoy the benefits of higher returns on their investments. The purpose of this government strategy is two-fold. On the one hand, it is good social policy, because average-income earners can in this way also accumulate capital. On the other hand it produces a better mix of creditors, so that as many people as possible commit themselves to the well-being of their country, a strategy which also reduces the government's dependency on corporate and foreign investors; (4) debt management has a stabilisation goal, i.e. debt management shall be used to balance the business cycle.

This may sound as if debt-management policies were only of a technical, non-political nature. It would, however, probably be fairer to say that general interest in debt-management policies is low, whereas the importance of these policies for governments should not be underestimated. The German federal government, for example, has to repay annually about one seventh of its debt total. This repayment is mostly credit-financed. It is remarkable that in the last few years a reduction of the total debt burden could be achieved, because interests on the old credits were 7 per cent whereas new money could be raised at an interest rate of merely 5 per cent (*Der Spiegel*, 28.4.1997: 28).

Limits for the public debt

The recent debate on deficits has confronted us with a paradox. On the one hand there is the opinion of economic experts who tell us that deficits today have reached dangerous proportions. Immediate action is said to be needed. On the other hand these experts cannot tell us when to act and how. Politicians who seek expert advice are therefore in an extremely difficult situation. They hear conflicting views, but what they need is some kind of strategy to control the development of deficits.

To cope with the growth of public debt three different approaches have emerged in OECD countries (Bach 1993). One strategy is to define categories of expenditures which can be financed by borrowed money. A central feature of such expenditures may be that they can be classified as investments, no matter how difficult an exact definition of investments may be. In contrast to consumption investments have two useful effects: one is that they create new assets which can be used by future generations. A second effect can be that investments are 'multipliers', i.e. they stimulate economic activities not only directly, but also indirectly in sectors of the economy which are in one way or the other connected with the sector of the economy where the investments were made.

A second strategy for the control of the deficit is the definition of an absolute limit the public debt may be allowed to reach. This limit is measured quantitatively by a certain economic category. An often used economic category for measuring the relative size of the annual deficit or the public debt is the GDP. Roy Jenkins, a former British Chancellor of the Exchequer and President of the European Commission, has often been cited with his dictum that public expenditure at some 60 per cent of GDP was of a calibre that causes danger to a 'plural society'. The 60 per cent debt-to-GDP ratio was chosen by the European Union when it was looking for a political compromise to define criteria for membership in the European Monetary Union in Maastricht in 1992.

A third debt control strategy tries to find procedural limits for the annual deficit. The idea behind this strategy is to erect extra hurdles for decisions on excessive (whatever the definition of excessive is) expenditures. Institutionalised limits for deficits help politicians to justify unpopular policies of financial restraint, because they are not a topic of party political controversy. This does not mean, however, that they are, as their defenders often claim, politically neutral. Extra hurdles for decisions on the deficit may make it more cumbersome to push through political priorities, but they are no firewall against strongly held political beliefs and are not immune to misuse. Such extra hurdles may be special (super)majorities needed for decisions on new deficits, the inclusion of additional institutions with veto powers in the decision-making process (such as the national banks), or an obligation for the government to inform the public each year in detail on its motives for overspending. The latter information can, of course, only have an effect on the size of the deficit if the public is interested in the issue and excessive deficits are widely regarded as a serious political and social problem (Gruber 1996: 159ff.). Rules can also be found for deficit-reduction strategies, for example by legislation on the speed and amount of expenditure cuts.

Notes

1. The term PSBR is used in a wide meaning for the amount of money borrowed annually by governments. This does not imply that PSBR data for different nations are comparable, because the definition of the public sector and accounting conventions vary. For details on the definition of the PSBR see Heald 1983: 41ff. In 1998 in Britain PSBR has been renamed the public sector net cash requirement, probably to distance it from the idea that cash alway comes from borrowing.

2. Obviously there have been periods in recent history in which tax rises have been regarded as something positive (the justification was the evolution of the welfare state), or in which expenditure cuts were seen as something preferable (for example to reduce the role of the state in the economy).

References

Alesina, Alberto and Perotti, Roberto (1995) *The Political Economy of Budget Deficits*, IMF Staff Papers, vol. 42(1), Washington, D.C.: IMF.

Bach, Stefan (1993) 'Institutionelle Beschränkung der Staatsverschuldung', in: *Konjunkturpolitik* 39 (1/2), pp. 1–27.

Barth, Hans J. (1981) 'Potentialorientierte Verschuldung. Das Konzept des Sachverständigen- rates zur Begutachtung der gesamtwirtschaftlichen Entwicklung', in: Diethard B. Simmert and Klaus-Dieter Wagner (eds): *Staatsverschuldung kontrovers*, Köln: Verlag Wissenschaft und Politik, pp. 58–70.

Bickley, James F. (1985) 'The Federal Financing Bank. Assessment of its effectiveness and budgetary status, in: *Public Budgeting and Finance* 5, pp. 51–63.

Buchanan, James M. and Wagner, Richard E. (1977) *Democracy in Deficit: The Political Legacy of Lord Keynes*, New York: Academic Press.

Doern, G. Bruce, Maslove, Allan M. and Prince, Michael J. (1988) *Public Budgeting in Canada*, Ottawa: Carleton UP.

Domar, Evsey D. (1944) ' "The Burden of the Debt" and the National Income', in: *American Economic Review* 34, pp. 798–827.

Downs, Anthony (1959–60) 'Why the government budget is too small in a democracy', in: *World Politics* 12, pp. 541–63.

Gantner, Manfried (1994) *Budgetausgliederungen – Fluch(t) oder Segen?*, Wien: Manz.

Gruber, Thomas (1996) *Rechtliche Schranken für staatliche Haushaltsdefizite*, Frankfurt am Main: Lang.

Heald, David (1983) *Public Expenditure*, Oxford: Martin Robertson.

Ibbolson, Roger G. and Sinquefield, Rex A. (1983) *Stocks, Bonds, Bills and Inflation, 1926– 1982*, Charlottesville, Va.: Financial Analysts Research Foundation.

Keynes, John Maynard (1937) *The General Theory of Employment, Interest, and Money*, New York: Harcourt Brace Jovanovich.

Kohl, Jürgen (1985) *Staatsausgaben in Westeuropa. Analysen zur langfristigen Entwicklung der öffentlichen Finanzen*, Frankfurt am Main/New York: Campus.

Lane, Jan-Erik (1993) *The Public Sector. Concepts, Models and Approaches*, London: Sage.

Lerner, Abba P. (1983) 'Functional finance and the federal debt', in: *Social Research* 10 (February), pp. 38–51.

Musgrave, Richard (1959) *The Theory of Public Finance. A Study in Public Economy*, New York: McGraw-Hill.

Newman, Herbert E. (1968) *An Introduction to Public Finance*, New York: John Wiley.

O'Connor, James (1973) *The Fiscal Crisis of the State*, New York: St Martin's.

OECD (1990) *Wirtschaftsberichte Vereinigte Staaten*, Paris: OECD.

Pampel, Ralf (1993) *Finanzinnovationen im Debt Management*, Wiesbaden: Deutscher Universitätsverlag.

Pliatzky, Leo (1982) *Getting and Spending. Public Expenditure, Employment and Inflation*, Oxford: Basil Blackwell.

Reich, Robert B. (1997) *Locked in the Cabinet*, New York: Alfred A. Knopf.

Schlesinger, Helmut, Weber, Manfred and Ziebarth, Gerhard (1993) *Staatsverschuldung – ohne Ende? Zur Rationalität und Problematik des öffentlichen Kredits*, Darmstadt: Wissenschaftliche Buchgesellschaft.

Schumpeter, Joseph A. (1942) *Capitalism, Socialism and Democracy*, New York and Lon- don: Harper.

Sharpe, William F. and Alexander, Gordon J. (1990) *Investments*, 4th edition, Englewood Cliffs, N.J.: Prentice Hall.

Smith, Adam (1976 edn) *An Inquiry into the Nature of Causes and the Wealth of Nations*, edited by Edwin Canaan, Chicago: University of Chicago Press.

Stockman, David A. (1986) *The Triumph of Politics. The Crisis in American Government and how it Affects the World*, London: Bodley Head.

Sturm, Roland (1989) *Haushaltspolitik in westlichen Demokration*, Baden-Baden, Nomos.

Tobin, James (1984) 'A Keynesian view of the budget deficit', in: *California Management Review* 26 (no. 2), pp. 7–14.

Wagner, Adolph (1911) 'Staat (in nationalökonomischer Sicht)', in: *Handwörterbuch der Staatswissenschaften*, 3rd edition, vol. VII, Jena: Fischer, pp. 727–39.

Wagschal, Uwe (1996) *Staatsverschuldung. Ursachen im internationalen Vergleich*, Opladen: Leske + Budrich.

Wildavsky, Aaron (1988) *The New Politics of the Budgetary Process*, Glenview (Ill.): Scott, Foresman, Little Brown.

Chapter 2

Britain

The history of the deficit problem

The post-war welfare state

In 1939, before Britain became involved in the Second World War, the country had foreign debts of £496 million and vast reserves in gold, dollars, and overseas investments. By 1945 it had lost these assets and its overall debt had grown to £3.5 billion (Childs 1979: 23). These pressures on the budget were largely responsible for a long period of austerity politics under the Labour Prime Minister Clement Attlee (1945–51). The balance of payments problems which plagued Britain even after the financial consequences of the Second World War had come under control remained difficult to manage. The major problem for Britain's economic development, the chronic imbalance of exports and imports due to the low productivity and the relative lack of competitiveness of British industry, contributed to the country's balance of payments problems.

The vicious circle of inadequate investments, low productivity, loss of foreign markets with the effect of reduced profits and a lack of investment capital also had consequences for national economic strategies. The appetite of consumers in the post-war years for imported products could not be matched by British exports. And for the rising expectations of citizens with regard to social consumption the national income was neither stable nor big enough. There was, however, a widespread belief among political decision-makers of all party political persuasions that Keynesian politics of macro-economic growth management would eventually yield the results necessary to bring about economic prosperity and to finance costly social policies. The Conservative Government of 1951 'tended to follow the "reformed" Keynesian Treasury line' (Ham 1981: 85). In 1954 the then Chancellor of the Exchequer, R.A. Butler, committed his government to doubling the national standard of living in the next twenty years.

The development of the welfare state in post-war Britain did not, however, turn around the country's economic fate. On the contrary, the gap between public income and expenditures widened even further. From 1957 onwards a sharp rise in

Table 2.1 PSBR as % of GDP

(a)		(b)	
1963	3	1980	3.4
1964	3	1981	2.6
1965	3	1982	2.5
1966	2	1983	3.3
1967	5	1984	4.0
1968	3	1985	2.8
1969	−1	1986	2.4
1970	0	1987	1.3
1971	2	1988	−1.1
1972	3	1989	−1.2
1973	6	1990	0.7
1974	8	1991	2.8
1975	10	1992	6.2
1976	7	1993	7.7
1977	4	(c)	
1978	5	1994	5.3
1979	6	1995	4 (forecast)

Sources: (a) Thompson 1986: 16; (b) Rajah and Smith 1994: 292; (c) OECD 1996: 26.

the trend of public expenditure is observable (Wright 1981: 7). All governments before Margaret Thatcher's first cabinet of 1979 found it easier to accept more spending than to raise taxes substantially. Ursula Hicks (1968: 315) argued that 'the combined effects of local authority, nationalized industry and the pressing needs of defence produced (from about 1962) a situation in which public sector expenditure exceeded what the resources of the country justified'. Overspending regularly provoked inflation and was counterbalanced by cut-back policies. Cut-backs then produced the unwanted result of large-scale unemployment which made governments, especially in pre-election periods, opt for greater expenditures.

None of these U-turns reduced the overall debt of the country, though the annual PSBR varied cyclically, and in 1969 and 1970 the budget was financed without the need for a deficit. Seen in perspective in a period of a relatively stable tax system from the 1950s to 1975 public expenditure in volume terms more than doubled whereas the GNP grew at a much slower rate (Wright 1981: 7). Still, in the context of the 1950s and 1960s in international comparison the lack of relative economic success seemed to be less dramatic, because both the world economy and the British economy were still growing at record rates. The PSBR only became an important concept in political debate in the mid-1970s (Thompson 1986: 15). In the 1950s and 1960s the term was hardly heard of. In the last year of the 1964–70 Labour Government the then Chancellor, Roy Jenkins, had even presented a balanced budget. The simple reason why in the 1970s the PSBR became an issue in its own right was that for British governments it had become an ever greater problem to finance it.

The Stop and Go cycle of political intervention to steer the British economy was interrupted neither by the efforts of the first Wilson Government of 1964, who had hoped to rejuvenate the British economy with the help of a technological revolution, nor by the economic fresh start in the early days of the Conservative Government of Edward Heath (after 1970). In the first Heath years the general aim of government policies was to free the market forces by a reduction of the power of the unions and a partial dismantling of the welfare state. However, strong social forces, not least the trade unions, prevented a radical change of the Keynesian logic of economic decision-making and defended what they regarded as the benefits of the welfare state. Instead of a reduction of the financial burden for the annual budget by expenditure cuts additional obligations were accepted by the governments of the 1970s.

One category of these very costly new obligations were the 'lame-duck' enterprises, uncompetitive firms which were nationalised to keep them alive and to save thousands of jobs. The all-party consensus on this kind of social policy was demonstrated by the 1971 decision of the Conservative Government of Edward Heath to rescue Rolls-Royce and Upper Clyde Shipbuilders. After nationalisation lame-duck enterprises remained unprofitable and dependent on public funds. Their considerable deficits had to be financed by the state in the limits set by the annual budget (External Financing Limits) and contributed to the annual PSBR.

Britain reacted to the oil crisis of 1973–4 with an even stronger dose of Keynesianism than had been applied before. The Labour Government relied on government spending to modernise and revitalise the economy and on a 'policy of "borrowing through" the oil deficit problem' (Ham 1981: 107). The then Chief Secretary of the Treasury (minister responsible for public expenditure) reports that 'the Chancellor had made the fundamental decision to react to the oil crisis in a different way from the German and Japanese, and indeed from many other developed countries. Instead of cutting expenditure to take account of the massive oil price increases of 1973, . . . the Chancellor decided to maintain our expenditure plans and borrow to meet the deficit' (Barnett 1982: 23).

The deficit was used as a counter-cyclical instrument. It rose at the time when output fell as a result of the recession in order to stimulate demand. Domestic production failed to recover, however. In the eyes of the Treasury 'what was disconcerting was the way in which projections of the PSBR turned out to be underestimated by a wide margin and had to be replaced by a succession of higher figures' (Pliatzky 1982: 131). The size of the budget deficit contributed to the erosion of the confidence of national and international markets in the stability of the pound which was threatened also by double-digit inflation rates and a gross imbalance of payments. In his March 1975 budget the Labour Chancellor of the Exchequer, Denis Healey, reacted by abandoning the post-war governments' commitment to plan for full employment. He concentrated his efforts on a reduction of the increase of the deficit. The new thinking of James Callaghan's Labour Government was neatly summarised in the Prime Minister's speech at the Labour Party Conference in 1976. It reads:

'We used to think that you could just spend your way out of recession and increase employment only by cutting taxes and boosting government expenditure . . . it only worked by injecting bigger doses of inflation into the economy followed by a higher level of unemployment at the next step. . . . The option no longer exists.'

(cited by Kavanagh 1987: 127)

In 1976 the Labour Government had to go to the International Monetary Fund for a loan to help refinance the national economy threatened by excessive government spending programmes (Rose and Karran 1987: 232). The 1976 loan forced the government of Prime Minister Callaghan to accept policies of spending cuts in order to fight inflation and to restore stability to the pound. The 1976 IMF loan was a turning point in British post-war economic history, because it forced the government to rethink its Keynesian strategies. This had the immediate result that the government tried to increase the element of corporatism, especially the role of the unions (for details see Taylor 1980: 150ff.), in its budgetary decision-making process in order to reduce the pressure for new expenditures. The year 1976 may have been an ideological turning point. However, it marked far less of a change with regard to the de facto control of the public debt.

Still, it is important to note that with the arrival of a new kind of economic thinking the government's attitude towards the PSBR changed. For the first time a British government announced economic target figures for the next four years which included targets for government borrowing. The PSBR was now to be reduced and public expenditure was to be better controlled. For the purpose of government decision-making on the budget the Chancellor, Denis Healey, therefore set a target figure for the PSBR, and this – in theory – determined all other decisions on the levels of taxation and public expenditure.[1] After the conditions for the IMF loan had been accepted, the PSBR could no longer be used as an instrument of Keynesian demand management. It became integrated into monetarist anti-inflation policies. In other words, the general aim of economic policies was now to control the deficit in order to control the money supply for the economy. An unchecked growth of the latter was identified as the major source of inflation. Thain (1992: 227) summarised this change in historical perspective:

> In the period from 1945 to 1973 governments of both major parties had reacted to rising unemployment with an active fiscal policy (increasing public expenditure or reducing taxation) and relaxing monetary policy. From 1975 an increase in unemployment produced a virtually neutral policy response. In no year after 1977 was the PSBR as a proportion of GDP as large as it was in 1974–75, despite the fact that unemployment rose to and remained at post-war historically high levels. In 1978 Healey [the Chancellor of the Exchequer] took action to reduce the PSBR when the financial markets became concerned that fiscal policy was out of step with monetary policy as the large PSBR was adding to monetary growth.

But in spite of its new economic strategies, the Labour Government still predominantly reacted to the development of the PSBR instead of conducting a planned attack on the deficit. This was reflected by several series of mini-budgets which corrected the original budget decisions and by the incrementalism of expenditure cuts. Whereas the Treasury already anticipated a radical change of policy in its suggestions to the Labour ministers, the latter were hesitant to follow its advise on expenditure cuts, and even Prime Minister James Callaghan was in an 'anti-Treasury mood' (Barnett 1982: 179). Not until the Conservative Government's 1980 Expenditure White Paper and the 1980–1 Financial Statement and Budget Report was there a published forecast of the PSBR (Heald 1983: 192).

Thatcherism, privatisation and North Sea oil

In contrast to the Labour Governments, Margaret Thatcher had a clear policy object-ive for the reduction of public expenditures. Although at first she felt 'boxed in' by previous expenditure decisions, especially on public sector pay policies, she was determined to 'make as vigorous a start as possible' (Thatcher 1993: 50). Over a four-year period from 1980 to 1984 she aimed at cuts in public expenditures of 4 per cent in real terms. In 1984 when confronted with the unplanned expenditure increases of the budget year 1982–3 the Conservative Government scaled down its policy objective from a further reduction in real terms to one of reducing public expenditure as a proportion of GDP. This objective was later changed again to the aim of holding the ratio constant (Thain and Wright 1992: 198).

With regard to deficit reduction policies Margaret Thatcher was from hindsight in one class with Ludwig Erhard, the German Economics Minister who was the brain behind that country's economic miracle. The Thatcher Governments success-fully controlled public expenditure levels at first in absolute terms. Later this was modified into the objective of holding the rate of growth of public expenditure below the rate of growth of the GDP. In Thatcher's case as in Erhard's it re-mains controversial how much of their respective success was their personal doing and how much of their success was quasi-automatically produced by some special circumstances of their time. It has been observed that 'the much-trumpeted fiscal surplus' was 'largely illusory' (Heald 1991: 80). And that 'Such presentation of the figures allowed the Conservative Government, after 1982 up to 1986, to run a mildly Keynesian fiscal policy at odds with its monetarist rhetoric' (Heald 1991: 93). Certainly statistical data as proof of success for economic strategies have to be viewed with a critical eye. A former Chief Secretary of the Treasury has confirmed the view that for office holders a certain amount of manipulation of budgetary data is a fairly easy exercise. He remarked (Barnett 1982: 22):

> I thought I had done a fair amount of juggling with figures as an accountant, but
> when it came to the sort of sophisticated 'massaging' and 'fudging' I learned as
> Chief Secretary, I realized I had been a babe in arms by comparison. It was a case of
> changing this and that 'assumption', and abracadabra – the Public Sector Borrowing
> Requirement (PSBR) is about the figure you first thought of!

It is undeniable that during the Thatcher years budgetary strategies found consider-able support by a source of income which has been described as 'fool's gold': a

Table 2.2 Total public-assets sales (incl. privatisation proceeds) in % of general government expenditure

1979–80	1.3
1980–1	1.3
1981–2	2.0
1982–3	2.3
1983–4	2.3
1984–5	3.1
1985–6	3.2
1986–7	4.4
1987–8	5.3
1988–9	7.2
1989–90	4.9

Source: Johnson 1991: 299.

£200 billion windfall profit from North Sea Oil (Harvie 1994). The oil was discovered in 1969. Because of the two oil crises of the 1970s which resulted in a sharp rise of the price of oil, British oil became competitive on the world market, and in the early 1980s its revenues began to fill the coffers of a Treasury run by a Conservative Government. Already in 1980 income from gas and oil production was £3.9 billion, and it reached £13.5 billion in 1985 (this was 12.6 per cent of total tax revenues) (Wolf 1986: 56).

Another factor which was unique for the Britain of the Thatcher and Major years was the privatisation of almost every state asset the markets would take. This policy had not been carefully planned. No White Paper on the economic strategy of which privatisation might have been a part was issued by the government. The most important motive for privatisation policies, at least in their early years, was an obvious and simple one. Privatisation proceeds were intended to help reduce the budget deficit. Not only did the Conservative Prime Ministers get rid of costly nationalised industries via privatisation. They could also control an important element of the PSBR by privatisations and a less generous policy with regard to expenditure limits for the nationalised industries, because – as mentioned above – subsidies to nationalised industries were included in the definition of public spending. The borrowing of public corporations amounted in most years between 1967 and 1979 to around 2 per cent of the GNP. In 1984 it had already shrunk to 0.3 per cent of the GNP (Eltis 1988: 77). In addition, privatisation generated huge amounts of additional state income. Over the period of 1980 to 1990 this new income was approximately £25 billion in 1990 prices (Rajah and Smith 1994: 286). In his memoirs Margaret Thatcher's first Chancellor, Sir Geoffrey, now Lord Howe (1994: 254), was very blunt about the need for such a strategy when commenting on his 1979–80 budget. He writes: 'The sensible disposal of public-sector assets had grown in urgency, not least as a short-term way of helping reduce the PSBR.'

The combined effects of North Sea oil and privatisations on the budgets of the Thatcher Governments was that for the first time in British post-war history a government was able to pay back money former governments had borrowed with the result of a genuine reduction of the public debt. Between 1987 and 1990 Britain had no need for an annual Public Sector Borrowing Requirement, but managed to create a budget surplus which the government used as a Public Sector Debt Reduction (PSDR) instrument. The country's debt-to-GDP ratio, which was 54.3 per cent in 1980 and even 60.4 per cent in 1984, both medium to high levels compared to other leading OECD countries, fell to 39.8 per cent in 1990 (Rajah and Smith 1994: 292).

John Major, who succeeded Margaret Thatcher in the office of Prime Minister after her resignation of 1990, inherited a 'balanced budget'. However, economic conditions changed dramatically in the early years of John Major's premiership. Oil prices fell and the budget income created by oil taxes was significantly reduced. Only a few state enterprises remained as potential candidates for privatisation, and the sale of most of them, such as British Rail or British Nuclear Fuels, did not promise much additional budgetary revenue. Budgetary pressures also grew, because the economic boom of the 1980s had ended, and Britain's economy was in deep recession. Annual GDP growth, which was still 2.3 per cent, in 1990 fell to 0.6 per cent in 1990 and turned negative in 1991 (–2.3 per cent) and 1992 (–0.4 per cent) (Rajah and Smith 1994: 285). The social consequences of the recession provoked an increase of government spending.

Research has shown, however, that the recession was not the only source for increased government spending. Another very important one was an increase of spending in virtually all programme categories, especially health, law and order, and transport (British Rail), a development which some argued reflected John Major's lack of 'political will' (Jenkins 1996: 229). Real programme expenditure grew at an annual rate of 0.6 per cent between fiscal year 1982–3 and fiscal year 1988–9, but by 4.0 per cent per year between fiscal year 1988–9 and fiscal year 1992–3 (OECD 1994: 45). In 1991 for the first time since 1987 the budget was again in deficit. Instead of the projected £7.9 billion for the PSBR, the PSBR even reached £13.7 billion. The main factor which drove up expenditures was increased payments to the unemployed due to the severe recession. In addition, local government self-financed expenditure was substantially increased (OECD 1993: 44). A problem also developed with regard to government income: the yield from taxes fell short of officials' estimates because the changes in the legislation on taxation, especially in corporate taxation, provoked errors in the forecasts of up to 10 per cent of the total deficit (Hogg and Hill 1995: 201f.).

In any event, John Major's spending policies reversed the trend to an ever smaller net general government debt as per cent of the GDP. From its record low in 1990 of 39.8 per cent government debt began to rise fast. The public debt-to-GDP ratio increased to 45.7 per cent in 1992 and reached the pre-1987 level of over 50 per cent in 1993 (51.9 per cent) (Rajah and Smith 1994: 285). The impetus to control a further increase of the public debt-to-GDP ratio came primarily from Chancellor Kenneth Clarke who sought to keep open for Britain the option of membership in the European Monetary Union. This implied that he tried (and he did so successfully) to keep the budget in the framework defined by the Maastricht criteria, even on the eve of the general election in 1997 when Eurosceptics and other party politicians would have preferred dramatic tax cuts in order to improve the attractiveness of John Major's Government in the eyes of the voters.

The institutional framework for decisions on the deficit

Britain is unique in that its system of government lacks any efficient mechanism which might control government spending policies – be it an institution outside government or a set of rules not controlled by the government. This is due to the fact that British constitutional and political realities now allow the Prime Minister a quasi-presidential role (Foley 1993) and what is more, a position in which he or she is 'accountable to none' (Jenkins 1996). Certainly the old doctrines of 'parliamentary sovereignty' and the 'rule of law' still apply. Parliament today is dominated by the House of Commons. In the latter the party of government controls most of the business and makes the decisions. The leader of the majority party is the British Prime Minister. Her or his policies thus find regular support in the House of Commons (Judge 1993). A successful parliamentary challenge to the government's budget (i.e. one that is also supported by MPs of the Prime Minister's own party) would almost certainly bring down the government of the day, forcing new elections.

What is excluded in such a system of decision-making on budgetary alternatives is a bargaining process between government and opposition which aims at winning over opponents and ends in an all-party compromise or the support of such a compromise by a temporary cross-party alliance. Parliament is not even allowed to initiate increases in taxes or expenditures. Ian Harden's conclusion (1989: 10) summarises the current state of affairs in a nutshell:

> The British fiscal constitution has a stark formal simplicity. The government proposes; the Commons assent to the proposals; the proposals are then enacted as legislation. All the battles, deals, lobbying and compromises happen in the privacy of the Executive branch of government, before the formal Parliamentary stage of proceedings.

How she or he wants to deal with the deficit problem remains the decision of the Prime Minister in office. The Prime Minister can also choose procedures of expenditure control which best suit her or his political intentions. Another important aspect of expenditure and tax policies in Britain is the high degree of centralisation of the budget. Local government is today reponsible for less than 10 per cent of government expenditures. The larger share is controlled by national law. Almost the same is true for the tax side of the budget. Local government taxes finance only about 18 per cent (Jenkins 1996: 42) of local government's expenditures.

Another aspect of the centralisation of public finances is that social services, e.g. the health service, are not financed by self-governing insurance systems into which employers and employees pay contributions and which therefore run their deficits independently from the national budgets. In Britain social policies are mostly tax-financed. The national insurance contributions (NIC) which are paid by employers, employees and the self-employed create entitlements to national insurance benefits.

The system is, however, not run on a strict insurance basis. Most commentators regard the NIC as a tax (Rajah and Smith 1994: 291). Social policy decisions with financial consequences (including health insurance) are a part of the annual budget decision. No special off-budget funds which may complicate deficit control policies exist. From a comparative point of view it can be said that the almost complete centralisation of budgetary decisions in Britain provides the government of that country with the most efficient institutional tools for controlling the national deficit and for securing the success of cut-back strategies of all the countries to be studied in this book.

Furthermore, institutional arrangements in Britain confer enormous discretion upon the government through control of information flows. Pre-budget information is only available to a small inner circle of people on a 'budget list' compiled by the Treasury, a list which does not automatically include Cabinet ministers. Insiders tell us that 'papers circulate in special orange folders containing numbered copies overprinted with warnings' (Hogg and Hill 1995: 193). The debate about deficit-reduction policies is, as David Heald observed (1995: 236), 'characterized by minimal hard information; over-the-top speculation by opposition parties; news stories planted by kite-flying ministers; and leaks of government documents and correspondence, some attributable to delivery agencies or dissident civil servants, but many leaked with ministerial authorization or connivance'. This enhances in the final analysis the power of government. It adds control over information to the government's control over procedures.

So, as was stressed by Rajah and Smith (1994: 305):

> from an institutional point of view the UK appears to be relatively well-placed to prevent the emergence of large-scale structural public sector deficits. The UK system involves a high degree of central control, with little decentralization, either within central government, or to lower levels of government. The political process in the UK allows government to keep tight control of initiatives for public spending and taxation; individual politicians outside the government are not permitted to propose tax or spending measures. The electoral system in the UK has the merit that it normally delivers stable governments, in office for a period of some four years, and able to count on political support within Parliament for decisive measures during this period.

The absence of efficient mechanisms of expenditure control which are independent from government does, of course, not prevent the government itself from creating its own internal control system. Situated in the centre of the deficit-control system of the British Government is the Treasury. The Treasury is the gate-keeper with regard to expenditure policies. Treasury control means at least limitation and constraint and at times reduction of expenditures (Thain and Wright 1992: 203; Thain and Wright 1995).

The debt crisis in perspective

The welfare consensus[2] of the post-war years, which was demonstrated by the commitment of the Conservative Government of Macmillan in the late 1950s to expand the public sector even at the price of the resignation of his Chancellor, Peter Thorneycroft, and two junior ministers at the Treasury, Enoch Powell and Nigel Birch, provided favourable conditions for expenditure policies. Until the mid-1970s the prevalent belief among the decision-makers in British governments was that public expenditure should not only be used for financing social expenditures, but also as an economic regulator. Deficits could help the economy along in times of crises whereas a reduction of public expenditures would dampen inflationary pressures. In other words, for the prevailing Keynesianism deficits had an economic function to fulfill. Deficits were not regarded as a force which causes economic distortion or which in the long run contributes to a severe national debt problem.

Much changed in the mid-1970s. In 1975–6 when public expenditure was rising towards 50 per cent of GDP, precipitating the IMF crisis, the Treasury's reaction to the loss of control of public spending had far-reaching consequences. As Jenkins (1996: 243f.) wrote:

> The Treasury's need to control public spending was the engine, the car and the fuel. For a decade and a half this was the vehicle that roared from one part of the public sector to another, destroying cosy relationships, protocols, concordats and many a racket. Complex treaties hallowed by decades of custom and practice were disregarded: treaties with the police, the schools, the universities and local government. Tight limits on spending and borrowing, on staffing and investment, on policy and practice transformed public-sector management.

Margaret Thatcher's understanding of monetarism, which became the guideline for the government's official economic policy after 1979, completely redefined the role of the deficit. For her the PSBR was 'an undesirable source of money creation, and tax cuts could be financed only by even larger public expenditure reductions' (Johnson 1991: 78). The latter were important because they were supposed to stimulate the economy and to restore its competitiveness. The fight against the deficit was seen as a fight against inflation. The objective of steadily reducing the PSBR as a percentage of GDP was chosen to facilitate the achievement of monetary targets with less pressure on the private sector through high nominal interest rates (Heald 1983: 51). Once the fight against the deficit was won, the public sector would stop 'crowding out' private investors. Interest rates for borrowing would go down, if the permanent high demand of the Treasury for new funds and the connected borrowing on the financial markets were brought to an end.

The logic of these arguments has created controversies among economists. Even Milton Friedman, the founder of 'monetarism', questioned the role assigned to PSBR by the anti-inflation strategy of Margaret Thatcher's Government. Maximilian Hall (1983: 96) warned early on against too much optimism with regard to the government's new instruments:

> Despite the public utterances of the government, one may conclude that the nature of the relationship between discretionary fiscal policy and the PSBR on the one hand and between the PSBR, interest rates and changes in £M3 on the other, are so complex as to deny to the authorities the ready availability of a simple rule of thumb that indicates how fiscal policy should be adjusted so as to ensure that the size and structure of the PSBR remain compatible with the stated monetary target. This poses an almost

unbearable burden on practitioners who seek to use the PSBR, cyclically adjusted, inflation adjusted or otherwise, as a flexible instrument of monetary control, even in the medium to long term.

What counted politically was the symbolic role the PSBR now began to play, and the psychological effects the announcement of PSBR targets had on economic actors, including government departments. David Heald (1995: 232) has argued that a crucial factor for the successful fight of the British Government against deficits in the 1980s was the political determination of the government to cope with the debt crisis:

> Tight control of public expenditure in the 1980s owed far more to clarity of ideological purpose and to strong political leadership than to systems [of expenditure planning]. The expenditure blow-out [under Major] was a reflection of the dissipation of both factors in the early 1990s.

For Prime Minister John Major a balanced budget remained a medium-term goal. He had to live with a growing PSBR in his first years in office, because of an unexpectedly severe recession and expansionary tendencies of his early budgets, which he had permitted in order to make a political point in the pre-election period which was supposed to distinguish himself from his predecessor Margaret Thatcher. From her he had inherited the problem of the poll tax for which in 1991 he had to put together a costly relief package. John Major's policies in general still aimed, however, at a consolidation of the budget. In contrast to Margaret Thatcher, who made capital expenditure projects bear the brunt of reductions, including public-sector housing, roads, hospitals and other infrastructure programmes (Mullard 1993: xvi), he remained worried about expenditure cuts which might have the effect of strangling necessary public investments. Their size became a limit for reductions of the future PSBR. According to Mullard (1993: 226): 'The additional increases in public expenditure together with the increases to the PSBR confirmed the break with the Thatcher approach to public finance.' In its fiscal year 1994–5 budget the government defined as its Medium Term Financial Strategy 'to bring the PSBR back towards balance over the medium term, and in particular to ensure that when the economy is on trend the public sector borrows no more than is required to finance its net capital spending'. In 1996 the government of John Major forecast a balanced budget for the fiscal year 1999–2000.

Deficit control policies

Following the proposals made in the Plowden Report (Plowden 1961) centralised expenditure planning was introduced in the Treasury. It was expected to help avoid the 'stop–go' policies which had characterised the management of the economy in the 1950s (Wright 1980: 112). In the 1960s and 1970s the Treasury's Public Expenditure Survey Committee (PESC) was the major instrument of central government for controlling public expenditures (Wright 1980; Pollitt 1977). PESC Planning, which was introduced in 1961, was above all 'volume planning'. It collected information on ministerial spending priorities and provided the full picture of the programmes the government was willing to support. This kind of planning was a strategic exercise which judged programmes politically on their relative merits with regard to general government policies. The financial implications of such programme decisions were calculated with reference to constant prices. Such prices ignored inflation and confronted budget planners regularly with nasty surprises when it came to financing programmes in the real world. The period between 1968 and 1974 has been characterised as the period of the 'high noon' of PESC, in which (uncharacteristically) the Treasury presided over the rapid expansion of public expenditure caused by generous spending policies of both Labour and Conservative governments and the indexation of public expenditures against high rates of inflation. The years 1974–6 brought to the open the degree of crisis of control of public expenditures (Thain and Wright 1992: 203).

It is not surprising that confronted with double-digit inflation in the 1970s and the need for an intervention of the IMF, Prime Minister Callaghan's Government decided that it could not accept automatically the size of a deficit which civil servants calculated on the basis of, as the Treasury officials christened constant prices, 'funny money', instead of real costs. Nor could the government accept that it lacked the necessary financial information on programmes. To avoid run-away costs in future years the Callaghan Government introduced cash limits[3] for PESC programmes (Else and Marshall 1981). In principle cash limits meant that, 'when volume programmes for the year immediately ahead had been settled at constant prices, and were being translated into cash provisions at the prices of the day, a limit would be placed in advance on the price increases to be covered and the amount of cash to be provided' (Pliatzky 1982: 138).

Cash limits were not intended to become an instrument which might help avoid deficits. They were merely intended to serve as a device for putting the lid on expenditures. But even in this respect cash limits proved to be fairly inefficient. One problem was that cash limits were not applied universally. In 1976 there were cash limits only for two thirds of public expenditures. In addition, when applied they were technically only meant for one year. Government departments could always return to their earlier spending plans and in doing so could worsen the deficit problem. An even more important problem was that the government lacked the political will to stick to its cash limits when confronted with the brutal fact that record inflation threatened the substance of its programmes. Political support for the government in the House of Common was weak, its majority was dwindling. So it could ill afford drastic spending cuts and tended to use money set aside for the contingency reserve to finance cost overruns. It turned out that once certain expenditures had become incorporated into the PESC process it was difficult for the Treasury to get them out again. Cash limits frequently had to be revised, mostly to accommodate expenditure increases for specific programmes (Thain and Wright 1992: 201).

With the introduction of cash limits the role of the Contingency Reserve as part of the budget plan changed. Its original purpose was to finance unexpected expenditures, and for this purpose a certain sum was set aside. After 1976 the proportion of the expenditure total set aside as Reserve grew steadily, and it kept growing in the Thatcher years. Thain and Wright (1990a: 4) concluded that the Reserve 'is now used to finance not only unanticipated expenditure, but anticipated overspending. In other words, provision for overspending was explicitly acknowledged and incorporated into the [spending] plans. A tacit admission of the failure to control expenditure.'

Margaret Thatcher's Government changed priorities in expenditure policies. The PESC as an inter-departmental committee of Principal Finance Officers of different departments had already ceased to play a central role in expenditure planning. As a committee, it continued to meet until the early 1980s. From the mid-1980s the short name for expenditure planning changed from the acronym PESC to 'the Survey', meaning the Public Expenditure Survey (PES) (Thain and Wright 1990).

After 1979 political decisions were no longer guided by the need to finance certain programmes, but by the need to control public expenditures. Revenue determined expenditure levels. In other words, the first decision the government made was on budgetary totals: income, expenditure, PSBR, and only the following decisions dealt with expenditure details. From 1982 the system of cash limits was succeeded by a system of cash planning, i.e. planning in a fixed amount of £s. No longer was there any automatic adjustment in expenditure planning to the actual movement of public sector pay and to prices. The volume of expenditure became – in theory – a residual 'controlled' by the actual inflation rate.[4] In practice some allowance for unexpected inflationary tendencies was made, as was admitted by the Treasury after the first few years of the new practice in 1984.[5] This had the consequence that the more successful the government was in fighting inflation the greater was the room for expenditures on programmes.

The lack of transparency of this system was even more pronounced than the secrecy surrounding the older expenditure planning system. The government published a general inflation forecast, but it remained unclear how this translated into programme expenditures. As inflation was seen in the monetarist tradition as a direct result of the development of monetary aggregates, the Thatcher Government at first tried to steer the development of the money supply as part of its Medium-Term Financial Strategy (Thain 1985). Money-supply targets were paramount, projections for the PSBR were meant to support these targets.

Before privatisation started on a large scale Margaret Thatcher's Government tried to defend the External Financing Limits defined in the annual budget for the nationalised industries in order to control this source of budget deficits. By a policy of price increases for industries, such as gas, water and electricity, with monopolistic or oligopolistic market power, the government even succeeded in creating additional income which could be used to offset the losses of other nationalised industries. In 1987–8, for example, the total deficit of the nationalised industries was reduced by £1.3 billion, because of the profits made by the Post Office and the Central Electricity Generating Board (CEGB) (Thain and Wright 1990a: 2f.).

After a few years of experimenting with different monetary aggregates the Thatcher Government had to admit that the direction monetary aggregates would take was too difficult to predict. Their interpretation was also too complicated for a government which looked for a simple yardstick to measure the success of its policies. The PSBR seemed to have the combined advantages of simplicity and transparency. In the mid-1980s the size of the PSBR became the almost exclusive point of reference for budgetary decisions. By setting targets for the PSBR, the authorities sought to influence the interest rates required to meet the targets for controlling inflation via the control of the money supply. Budgeting aimed, in other words, simultaneously at sound finances (a balanced budget) and low inflation.

When the economic problems of the Major Government led to new public-sector deficits, the importance of the PSBR was officially scaled down. The government argued that the PSBR was just one instrument for monitoring the development of inflation, which in itself was a much more important economic indicator. Instead of the Old Planning Total of expenditures which was used between 1977 and 1989 and which was comprised of central government expenditure, local authority expenditure, the external financing of nationalised industries and of some public corporations, the budget reserve and privatisation proceeds, a New Planning Total which excluded local authority expenditure was announced in 1990. This reform lasted only till 1993. It was justified by the introduction of a new system of local government taxation, the community charge or 'poll tax' (for details see Butler, Adonis and Travers 1994), which reduced London's responsibility for local government expenditures. The New Planning Total did nothing, however, to improve the government's capacity for control of the PSBR. It had the advantage, however, of obscuring the size of the deficit problem in a pre-election period.

A more radical change in government accounting was provided by the introduction of the New Control Total (NCT) in 1993. The NCT was the government's response to a spiralling of the PSBR which in 1992 had also motivated the then Chief Secretary to the Treasury, Michael Portillo, to initiate a government-wide Fundamental Expenditure Review (FER) (Parry, Hood and James 1997). The essence of NCT is the idea that the Cabinet sets an annual global public expenditure limit which is absolutely binding. The Treasury and the spending departments negotiate the allocation of resources in the framework thus set. The way of calculating expenditure totals, which exclude cyclical social security,[6] debt interest and accounting adjustments,[7] remains unchanged. If a department secures for itself an increase of resources greater than the increase of the overall budget, the additional money needed to finance this increase has to be found in the budget of other departments. If this causes conflict, the Cabinet decides.

Though this reform was celebrated by the government as creating more transparency and as a system easier to run, it is obvious that it also provided a welcome solution for some other problems of public expenditure. The exclusion of privatisation proceeds which critics (for example the Treasury and Civil Service Committee of the House of Commons) had asked for, because they objected to seeing them treated as negative expenditure (Heald 1991: 78), owed more to the drying up of this sort of state income than to a genuine policy change.

In 1992 the process of arbitration between the demands of ministries for more funds and the Treasury's determination to defend expenditure limits was reformed. The annual ritual of the PES was given a new focus. Its old routine used to confront departmental horror stories of 'bleeding stumps', of vital tasks harmed by the Treasury's thrift, and the Treasury's totals, which showed how impossible it was to fulfill everybody's wishes. Until 1992 it was the Chief Secretary who was in the uncomfortable position of having to reach deals with his reluctant Cabinet colleagues. Now the Chancellor, Norman Lamont, and his Chief Secretary, Michael Portillo, took the initiative to shift this responsibility to a new Cabinet committee, the EDX, in order to strengthen the forces of the Treasury. Or in the language of two insiders (Hogg and Hill 1995: 120, fn.7):

> EDX . . . was packed with two kinds of Cabinet beasts; there were the heavyweights
> – the Prime Minister's A-team; and there were some supposedly disinterested
> Ministers with small departmental budgets. The former ensured that, when EDX's
> recommendations came to Cabinet, Treasury ministers could call up some big political
> guns in support. The point about the latter was that they could be persuaded to help
> fight the Treasury's battles by early offers of small change from the Chief Secretary's
> back pocket. So when other Ministers were summoned before the committee, one or
> other EDX member could be counted on to go for a colleague's jugular.

In October 1992 the government of John Major adopted an explicit inflation rate target. The government's main objective was at first to keep the underlying rate of inflation within a range of 1 to 4 per cent. To improve on the credibility of this target the government also increased the transparency of its policy decisions. The Bank of England was allowed to write quarterly reports on the progress made towards meeting the target. The Chancellor of the Exchequer and the Governor of the Bank of England had regular monthly meetings to discuss monetary policies. The minutes of these meetings were published with a time lag of about six weeks. In 1992 a panel of independent forecasters was established. The panel advised the Treasury. Its reports were published three times a year.

The control of the deficit was also expected to be made easier, at least technically, by the government's decision to present a unified budget in autumn, instead of an autumn statement on expenditures and a separate budget on taxes in March. The decision on taxes was still formally made in March, but since November 1993 a single document has brought together forecasts on both state income and expenditures. A further effort to control expenditures and indirectly the PSBR[8] was made with the 1995 decision to introduce Resource Accounting for the Public Expenditure Survey by the year 2000. Resource Accounting is defined by the Treasury as a set of accruals accounting[9] techniques for reporting on the expenditure of central government and a framework for analysing expenditure by departmental aims and objectives, relating these to outputs where possible (Likierman 1995: 563). It is expected to help control the PSBR because it provides the full picture over time, i.e. additional information, of expenditures in a way similar to business accounting.

After the election victory of the Labour Party in 1997 there has been talk of a possible end of the unified budget and a return to the old procedures. The over-all picture changed dramatically with the new government's decision to grant the Bank of England autonomy with regard to setting interest rates. The Labour Party in opposition had promised continuity of taxing and spending policies should the

Party win the election. Still, the philosophy behind New Labour's deficit control politics remained unclear. In a pre-election book Peter Mandelson, Minister and key figure in Tony Blair's Government, had supported old Keynesian views on the deficit. He wrote (Mandelson and Liddle 1996: 80):

> fiscal policy should be set in the context of a clear medium-term plan. This plan should abide by the golden rule of public finance: that current income and current expenditure should be in balance over the economic cycle. While public borrowing should rise and fall in order to help offset temporary fluctuations in economic activity, as Keynes argued it should, the only purpose for which an increase in long-term government debt would be permitted should be to finance public investment.

The first Labour budget of 1997 has shown what this statement meant in practice. The new Chancellor, Gordon Brown, repeated his earlier pledge to stabilise the debt-to-GDP ratio over the economic cycle. His budget aimed at annual deficit reductions over the next five years.

In its November 1997 pre-Budget report the government proposed a Code for Fiscal Stability which defined 'the golden rule' of budgeting. This rule implies that current expenditure will be covered by current revenues over the economic cycle or that the deficit will not be larger than investment (for further details see OECD 1998: 46f.). The latter requires all ministries to make a sharp distinction between spending on capital projects – such as new schools and hospitals – and current expenditure. By the year 2000 the Chancellor even expects the public sector to be a net repayer of debt (*The Economist*, 5.7.1997: 42). The Institute for Fiscal Studies (*Financial Times*, 25.1.98: 6) is only slightly less optimistic. Because of Britain's booming economy it expects a debt repayment of 1.4 per cent of GDP for the 2002–3 budget.

Deficits – the British experience

In Britain problems with the deficit seemed for a long time synonymous with structural weaknesses of the British economy. The Labour Party strategy of the 1970s to borrow in order to rejuvenate the country and to lead it out of its economic crisis produced, however, only greater deficits. Still, even in the 1980s, when the Conservatives led by Margaret Thatcher came to power, strategies to attack the deficit remained part of a wider framework of economic reform. No attempt was made to make deficit-reduction the only target of economic policies. The expectation was that radical economic reform, which included strict expenditure controls, would not only make the country more competitive, but would also restore sound budgets. The PSBR was watched closely as an indicator for the success of the government's fight against inflation, whose minimisation or elimination had become the single target of macro-economic policy (Wilks 1997: 689f.).

Margaret Thatcher succeeded in overcoming the deficit problem for a few years. This was, however, not only due to her cut-back policies, which were felt above all by the poorer strata of society. An important factor which also contributed to budgetary surpluses was the additional income from North Sea Oil and public

sector privatisations. After a short recession in the early 1990s, the economy returned to its course of recovery. Tony Blair inherited from John Major a booming
economy which will even allow the British Government to balance its budget again
in the upcoming years and to repay public debts.

It is typical for the British experience of budgeting that in exceptional circumstances ideological rigour in economic policies can be translated fairly easily into
efficient political intervention, because of the unchecked power of central government. So, the moment the government acknowledges that the deficit is a problem
which needs its attention, it can immediately rearrange its political priorities and its
policies, if the Prime Minister provides sufficient political leadership. The lack of
institutional checks on public spending outside the government forces the government to exercise a high degree of self-control if it wants to control the deficit. Self-
control means in institutional terms that the government arranges for internal control
mechanisms. With intransparent and fairly technical procedural changes in the
machinery of government and especially of the organisation of tax and expenditure
decisions in the Treasury and the Cabinet, British governments have time and again
tried to force ministers and bureaucrats to adhere to the government's general
budgetary goals. We have certainly not yet seen the end of such experiments, as the
new initiatives of Prime Minister Tony Blair's Labour Government demonstrate.

The aim of these procedural controls changed over time. The major difficulty
was at first seen in the problem of finding a 'rational' argument for the correct
amount of spending. The role of a neutral arbiter could perhaps be played by a
committee of non-spending ministers, for example, or of civil servants. In practice
spending remained, however, driven by expenditure needs. When in the context of
the IMF loan of 1976 stronger measures to control spending and by implication
to control the deficit became unavoidable, a shift of emphasis in expenditure control began. During Margaret Thatcher's time in office as Prime Minister, priorities
were rearranged. Spending was no longer defined by the need to finance political
projects. Political projects were now made dependent on the availability of funds.
This allowed the government to define to a great extent the size of net public
borrowing and to improve its control over the development of the public debt.

If we compare post-war Britain to the Britain of the 1980s and 1990s we can
observe that in the former deficits were seen as an instrument of governments for
coping with economic crises and for building up the welfare state. Today this is the
distant past. Deficits are now seen as unwanted restrictions for government politics.
Governments have in all countries we study here given up the idea that they should
be able to spend their way out of recession. The expansion of the welfare state is no
longer the overriding aim even of a British socialist government. The Blair Government accepts that its major aim in budgetary politics should be a balanced budget
and a reduction of the debt-to-GDP ratio. Recently, as has already long been the
case in Germany, the level of investments has officially become the yardstick for
the limit of annual government borrowing. And the government even went one step
further. To better control expenditures the annual spending decisions were abolished in 1998. Ministers' budgets will henceforth be set three years at a time –
similar to Canadian practice after the latest reforms.

Notes

1. In practice a lot of energy was invested in fiddling the PSBR figures; see: Barnett 1982: 124ff.

2. Contemporary historians have challenged the view that there was enough common ground between the Labour Party and the Tories, especially with regard to ideology, to talk about consensus. They would probably agree that 'consensus' is not a completely wrong description of policy outcomes though they might claim differences in intentions between the two major parties. See, for example: Kandiah 1996: 74.

3. The system was first explained to Parliament in the White Paper on 'Cash Limits in Public Expenditure' (Cmnd. 6440) of April 1976.

4. Critics remarked that cash planning was 'a blunt instrument of great appeal to those attaching priority to less rather than better spending' (Heald 1983: 196).

5. The Treasury adjusted all cash plans for inflation by one and the same general index of inflation, the GDP deflator. Unlike the Retail Price Index, this is a general measure of home costs and is not influenced by import prices or mortgage interest. It is intended to be an indication of what a programme is costing the Treasury to finance in real terms, by a general yardstick, rather than what level of real service output the programme is giving (Johnson 1991: 84).

6. Cyclical social security is defined as unemployment benefit and income support paid to people of working age. It is excluded from the NCT to ensure that in future periods of strong economic growth savings here are not considered to provide scope for higher spending.

7. Adjustments to national accounts concepts.

8. 'For the purposes of the PSBR, cash will be controlled in aggregate through the prescription of the Total Financial Requirement which will consist of the total cash required to finance departments' Resource Budgets, and the cash costs of those items excluded from the Resource Control Total, such as cyclical social security and debt interest' (Wright 1995: 584).

9. 'Accruals accounts record costs and revenues as they are respectively incurred and earned. By contrast, cash accounting records cash payments and receipts when they are made. An illustration of the difference is that under accruals accounting, the whole cost of a computer bought for cash and estimated to last for five years will be spread over the five years' (Likierman 1995: 563).

References

Barnett, Joel (1982) *Inside the Treasury*, London: André Deutsch.

Butler, David, Adonis, Andrew and Travers, Tony (1994) *Failure in British Government. The Politics of the Poll Tax*, Oxford: Oxford UP.

Childs, David (1979) *Britain Since 1945. A Political History*, London and New York: Methuen.

Else, P.K. and Marshall, G.P. (1981) 'The unplanning of public expenditure: recent problems in expenditure planning and the consequences of cash limits', in: *Public Administration* 59, pp. 253–278.

Eltis, Walter (1988) 'Britain's budget deficit in 1967–84: its consequences, causes and policies to control it', in: Cavanna, Henri (ed.), *Public Sector Deficits in OECD Countries. Causes, Consequences and Remedies*, Basingstoke and London: Macmillan, pp. 76–101.

Foley, Michael (1993) *The Rise of the British Presidency*, Manchester: Manchester UP.

Hall, Maximilian (1983) *Monetary Policy since 1971. Conduct and Performance*, Basingstoke and London: Macmillan.

Ham, Adrian (1981) *Treasury Rules. Recurrent Themes in British Economic Policy*, London: Quartet Books.

Harden, Ian (1989) *The Fiscal Constitution Under Stress*, Working Paper, University of Sheffield.

Harden, Ian (1995) 'Regulating government', in: *Political Quarterly* 66, pp. 299–306.

Harvie, Christopher (1994) *Fool's Gold. The Story of North Sea Oil*, London: Hamish Hamilton.

Heald, David (1983) *Public Expenditure*, Oxford: Martin Robertson.

Heald, David (1991) 'The political implications of redefining public expenditure in the United Kingdom, in: *Political Studies* 39, pp. 75–99.

Heald, David (1995) 'Steering public expenditure with defective maps', in: *Public Administration* 73, pp. 213–240.

Hicks, Ursula K. (1968) *Public Finance*, Cambridge: Cambridge UP.

Hogg, Sarah and Hill, Jonathan (1995) *Too Close to Call*, London: Little Brown.

Howe, Geoffrey (1994) *Conflict of Loyalty*, Basingstoke and London: Macmillan.

Hutton, Will (1996) *The State We're In*, London: Vintage.

Jenkins, Simon (1996) *Accountable to None. The Tory Nationalization of Britain*, Harmondsworth: Penguin.

Johnson, Christopher (1991) *The Economy under Mrs Thatcher 1979–1980*, Harmondsworth: Penguin.

Judge, David (1993) *The Parliamentary State*, London: Sage.

Kandiah, Michael (1996) 'Conservative leaders, strategy – and Consensus? 1945–1964', in: Jones, Harriet and Kandiah, Michael (eds), *The Myth of Consensus. New Views on British History, 1945–64*, London: Macmillan, pp. 58–78.

Kavanagh, Dennis (1987) *Thatcherism and British Politics. The End of Consensus?*, Oxford: Oxford UP.

Likierman, Andrew (1995) 'Resource accounting and budgeting: rationale and background', in: *Public Administration* 73, pp. 562–70.

Mandelson, Peter and Liddle, Roger (1996) *The Blair Revolution. Can New Labour Deliver?*, London and Boston: Faber and Faber.

Mullard, Maurice (1993) *The Politics of Public Expenditure*, 2nd edition, London and New York: Routledge.

OECD (1993) *Economic Surveys (United Kingdom)*, Paris: OECD.

OECD (1994) *Economic Surveys (United Kingdom)*, Paris: OECD.

OECD (1996) *Economic Surveys (United Kingdom)*, Paris: OECD.

OECD (1998) *Economic Surveys (United Kingdom)*, Paris: OECD.

Parry, Richard, Hood, Christopher and James, Oliver (1997) 'Reinventing the Treasury: economic rationalism or an econocrat's fallacy of control', in: *Public Administration* 75, pp. 395–415.

Pliatzky, Leo (1982) *Getting and Spending. Public Expenditure, Employment and Inflation*, Oxford: Basil Blackwell.

Plowden, Lord Edwin (1961) *Control of Public Expenditure*, London: HMSO (Cmnd 1432).

Pollitt, Christopher (1977) 'The Public Expenditure Survey 1961–72', in: *Public Administration* 55, pp. 127–42.

Rajah, Najma and Smith, Stephen (1994) 'Fiscal developments in the United Kingdom since 1980, in: *European Economy* 3, pp. 281–307.

Rose, Richard and Karran, Terence (1987) *Taxation by Political Inertia*, London: Allen & Unwin.

Taylor, Robert (1980) *The Fifth Estate. Britain's Unions in the Modern World*, 2nd edition, London: Pan Books.

Thain, Colin (1985) 'The education of the Treasury: the medium-term financial strategy 1980–84', in: *Public Administration* 63, pp. 261–85.

Thain, Colin (1992) 'Government and the economy', in: Jones, Bill and Robins, Lynton (eds), *Two Decades in British Politics*, Manchester: Manchester UP, pp. 221–42.

Thain, Colin and Wright, Maurice (1990) *The Public Expenditure Survey*, Working Paper No. 10 (= The Treasury and Whitehall: Public Spending and Control).

Thain, Colin and Wright, Maurice (1990a) 'Coping with difficulty. The Treasury and public expenditure', in: *Policy and Politics* 18(1), pp. 1–15.

Thain, Colin and Wright, Maurice (1992) 'Planning and controlling public expenditure in the UK, Part I and II', in: *Public Administration* 70, pp. 3–14 and pp. 193–224.

Thain, Colin and Wright, Maurice (1995) *The Treasury and Whitehall*, Oxford: Clarendon.

Thatcher, Margaret (1993) *The Downing Street Years*, London: Harper Collins.

Thompson, Grahame (1986) *The Conservatives' Economic Policy*, London: Croom Helm.

Wilks, Stephen (1997) 'Conservative governments and the economy, 1979–97', in: *Political Studies* 45, pp. 689–703.

Wolf, Gerd (1986) *Wechselseitige Beeinflussung von gesamtwirtschaftlicher Entwicklung und öffentlichem Haushalt. Ein Vergleich der Erfahrungen aus den Jahren 1970 bis 1985 im VK und in der BRD*, Bonn: Stollfuss (= Schriftenreihe des BMF, Vol. 37).

Wright, Maurice (1980) 'From planning to control: PESC in the 1970s', in: Wright, Maurice (ed.), *Public Spending Decisions. Growth and Restraint in the 1970s*, London: Allen & Unwin, pp. 88–119.

Wright, Maurice (1981) 'Big government in hard times: the restraint of public expenditure', in: Hood, Christopher and Wright, Maurice (eds), *Big Governments in Hard Times*, Oxford: Martin Robertson, pp. 3–31.

Wright, Maurice (1995) 'Resource budgeting and the PES system', in: *Public Administration* 73, pp. 580–90.

Chapter 3

Canada

The history of the deficit problem

The rise and fall of expenditure planning

As in Britain, in Canada the deficit problem did not arrive until the 1970s and developed into a serious political and economic concern in the early 1980s. In the post-war decades Canada went through two major phases of budgetary change (Doern, Maslove and Prince 1988: 47ff.). The first period can even be traced back to the early 1930s. Its characteristic is that the then dominant budgetary norm was that of balanced budgets, a norm which was valid well into the 1960s. With regard to expenditure decisions the most important institutional actor in this period was the Minister of Finance. Expenditure was tightly controlled, because legislation provided for the approval of every single item of expenditure by the Comptroller of the Treasury. Still, first efforts of macro-economic Keynesian management of the economy were made. At the centre of budgeting were the budgetary 'inputs', such as personnel or equipment. The absence of any major economic crisis in the post-war years made it possible to finance these 'inputs' without the need for borrowing money. Between 1947 and 1951 substantial budget surpluses were accumulated (Strick 1985: 164). Between 1950 and 1975 strong economic growth reduced the federal debt, when measured as a proportion of GDP, although in absolute figures it was growing.

Table 3.1 The debt problem: net public debt, the federal deficit (both in % of GDP) (1) and public debt charges (federal budget in % of expenditures)

	Net public debt	Annual deficit or surplus (+)	Net public debt charges
1926–7	45.6	+0.8	36.7
1931–2	50.6	2.4	26.9
1936–7	66.6	1.7	35.3
1941–2	48.3	4.3	8.2
1946–7	106.6	+3.6	15.4
1951–2	48.0	+1.6	10.5

	Net public debt	Annual deficit or surplus (+)	Net public debt charges
1956–7	35.7	+1.0	5.7
1957–8	34.7	0.6	5.6
1958–9	36.0	2.5	6.4
1959–60	35.6	1.7	7.9
1960–1	35.6	1.4	7.3
1961–2	35.7	2.3	7.1
1962–3	34.7	1.9	8.0
1963–4	34.8	2.5	7.6
1964–5	32.4	0.6	7.3
1965–6	28.9	+0.5	7.8
1966–7	26.1	0.3	6.7
1967–8	25.4	1.0	5.9
1968–9	23.7	0.5	6.2
1969–70	21.2	+0.4	6.0
1970–1	20.6	0.9	5.7
1971–2	20.5	1.6	5.4
1972–3	19.9	1.5	5.0
1973–4	18.5	1.6	4.5
1974–5	16.8	1.3	4.6
1975–6	18.3	3.3	5.1
1976–7	19.0	3.2	5.7
1977–8	22.0	4.8	6.5
1978–9	25.1	5.2	8.0
1979–80	26.1	4.2	9.1
1980–1	27.6	4.4	10.2
1981–2	28.2	4.2	13.4
1982–3	34.3	7.4	13.9
1983–4	39.6	8.0	14.2
1984–5	44.8	8.6	16.7
1985–6	48.8	7.2	19.5
1986–7	52.3	6.1	19.3
1987–8	53.1	5.1	19.5
1988–9	53.4	4.8	20.9
1989–90	55.1	4.4	27.1
1990–1	58.4	4.8	27.7
1991–2	62.9	5.1	25.5
1992–3	67.6	6.0	24.1
1993–4	71.3	5.9	23.3
1994–5	72.8	5.0	
1995–6	74.2	3.7	
1996–7(2)	74.8	2.0	

(1) For 1926–7 to 1960–1 inclusive, figures are expressed as percentage of GNP. (2) estimated
Sources: For 1926–7 to 1988–9, Minister of Finance, *The Budget*, Ottawa: Department of Finance 1990, p. 148 and OECD 1997: 34.

In the period from the early 1960s to the early 1970s the Canadian budgetary process was adjusted on a broader scale to the more ambitious project of state interventionism. Bakker (1990: 426) believes, however, that the Keynesian welfare state was never warmly embraced in Canada. It was 'tolerated as long as it was financed out of increased economic growth and higher marginal incomes; it was deemed acceptable and muted distributional conflicts between capital and labour.' On the one hand Keynesian macro demand management was strengthened. On the other hand new planning techniques became accepted which concentrated more on the output of budgeting than the input. Institutionally, a greater stress on macro-economic management meant a separation of the Treasury Board with its own president from the Department of Finance. Whereas the day-to-day management of the government's expenditure policies was entrusted to the Treasury Board, the Department of Finance became the planner of general economic trends.

The new form of budgetary planning was at first a political reaction to the Glassco Royal Commission report. The report had criticised the detailed input controls of the Ministry of Finance. It had argued that budgeting might be a more efficient exercise if the different ministries would run their departments like businesses. The basic idea was that in the corridors of public administration the management potential existed, and that it was the responsibility of the government to 'let the managers manage'. This management orientation of expenditure policies was further strengthened by the introduction of elements of programme planning in the Ministry of Finance. Between 1969 and 1977 bureaucrats tried in vain to improve on the efficiency of spending programmes and to define single expenditure items which were adequate for different steps of the budgetary planning process. The new management techniques, which were mostly transfers from similar exercises in the United States, could not overcome basic problems of budgetary planning, such as the lack of information, the time pressure under which budgetary decisions must be made, or the fact that a budget decision always involves settling a conflict between competing interests and is not sufficiently aloof politically to be decided by bureaucratic reasoning alone.[1]

The period from the early 1970s to 1982 has been characterised as one 'in which there was a grudging and belated rediscovery of scarcity' (Doern and Phidd 1992: 139). The debate on the deficit began in Canada after the world wide oil crisis in 1974–5, though not with an immediate impact on Canadian Government policies. The slowdown in economic growth after 1975, which was accompanied by budget deficits, started the trend which led to a growing debt problem. Strick (1985: 177) has summarised the policy dilemma of Keynesianism at that time:

> The sizeable budget deficits being incurred annually were caused by a combination of developments. Rising costs produced an automatic increase in government spending on established programs; a sluggish economy, together with the indexing of the personal income tax, reduced the rate of increase in government revenues. The deficits provided an expansionary impact on the economy as a whole. However, with inflationary pressures continuing, the desire to avoid further increases in an already substantial deficit ruled out massive additional expenditure for employment-creating programs.

In 1979 tight monetary policy by the Bank of Canada as a reaction to a policy change in the US Federal Reserve pushed up interest rates and therefore the cost of debt services. Higher interest rates also affected the Canadian economy as a whole. The recession which finally resulted in 1981–2 caused dramatic increases in the deficit and a rapid accumulation of federal debt (Carmichael 1984: 5).

The monetarist 'counter-revolution' (Donner and Peters 1979) in economic thought, which led to a reorientation of the Bank of Canada's economic philosophy in 1975, at first criticised the limits and failures of Keynesian macro-economic management, especially its inability to cope with stagflation (simultaneous occurrence of economic stagnation and inflation). The monetarists argued that part of the economic damage done was due to an excessive role of the state in the economy. They criticised big government borrowing which crowded out private investors,[2] because government borrowing caused higher than necessary interest rates on capital markets. The fiscal policy goal derived from this argument was to restrain federal spending with the objective of reducing its share of GNP. In addition to a general critique of state interventionism, the deficit as such started to attract greater attention. The driving force behind the massive increase of the deficit in the 1970s was not only reduced public income, caused by the recession. In the mid-1970s Canada had also introduced policies which prevented the budget from gaining additional tax income through high inflation, such as indexed tax brackets, personal income tax exemptions and indexed social assistance payments. In other words, in these cases inflation was neither creating a greater tax income, nor was it devaluing social expenditures.

The debate on the deficit, which reached the decision-making process of the Canadian Government at the end of the 1970s, stressed the problems of expenditure policies which tended to get out of control and of the growing importance of resources needed to finance the annual debt service (Butler and Macnaughton 1984). The Liberal Trudeau Government argued that expenditure policies should be made dependent on economic growth, but it did not end a strategy of budgeting which gave priority to programmes over financial limitations. In a belated reaction to political pressures Prime Minister Trudeau ordered a two-billion dollar expenditure cut in August 1978, which was, however, exercised without any effect on the general thrust of budgeting. This cut has been described as a 'prime ministerial "lightning bolt"', which hit at a time when most ministers were on vacation (Doern and Phidd 1992: 145). Perceptions of the deficit problem remained divorced from public expenditure control. Expenditure cuts were above all meant to be anti-inflationary policies. As late as 1979 the Canadian Tax Foundation published a study which came to the conclusion (Bird 1979: 55): 'For the moment . . . it seems safe to say that anyone worrying unduly about the growth of the public debt in Canada is for the most part wasting his time.'

Prime Minister Joe Clark's short-lived Progressive–Conservative minority Government of 1979 tried to find a new strategic response to cope with the lack of resources for new expenditures. The new government announced 10 per cent expenditure cuts for the coming four years and a reduction of total expenditures from 21 per cent of GDP (1979) to 18 per cent GDP (1983).

Trudeau's return to power in 1980 postponed, however, a change of budgetary direction. Trudeau's Third National Policy was a last effort to use the country's resources to create socio-economic stability, though not necessarily social redistribution. Doern and Phidd (1992: 147) have noted that: 'In terms of resource allocation the Liberal expenditure plans gave a clear indication, if carried out, that economic development would receive the top priority, and social expenditures would be given a low priority.' Trudeau's policies gave priority to programmatic change; fiscal limits remained of secondary importance. Minister of Finance, Allan MacEachen, officially committed the government to expenditure increases no greater than the growth of GNP and to a gradual reduction in the deficit, but without major tax increases. It was hoped that the success of the government policies would also solve the deficit problem. A typical example for the thrust of Trudeau's policies is the National Energy Program (NEP) which subsidised consumers in central and eastern Canada by below world market oil prices, as had already been the case in 1973. This was a major factor which contributed to the virtual doubling of the federal deficit in the 1979 to 1981 period (Doern, Maslove and Prince 1988: 207).

A new problem was created in the 1970s by the plethora of tax expenditures, subsidies which had the double effect of pleasing interest groups and of strategic incentives for the Keynesian demand management of the economy. Savoie (1990: 323) illustrates this point. He writes: 'It will be recalled that tax expenditures were viewed as free money and "more easily accessible" and that by 1985 it was estimated that Ottawa had over 300 tax expenditure items, compared with 200 in 1980.' Others argue that from the mid-1970s until the 1982–3 recession federal spending was well under control, and that the deficit was caused above all by revenue shortfalls (Doern *et al.* 1988: 207; Bakker 1990: 425; Wolfe 1985: 121):[3] 'Key policy changes, such as the decision in 1974 to index the income-tax system, explain, along with a small handful of other tax expenditures, much of the increasing loss of billions of revenue dollars' (Doern *et al.* 1988: 207). A further loss of revenue was provoked by the fact that the government had been forced to reduce its taxes on petroleum as international oil prices began to fall. Up to 1984 the effects of recession and in its aftermath expansionary fiscal policies led to a sizeable increase of the federal deficit (OECD 1988: 12).

The Clark Government of 1979–80 had established an envelope system of budgeting, the Public Expenditure Management System (PEMS), as it was officially called, which can be regarded as the last effort to rescue budgeting from the mere logic of muddling through. The system assigned blocks of expenditure (envelopes) to different Cabinet committees. The envelope 'Economic Development', for example, brought together the ministerial responsibilities for industry and technology; agriculture, fisheries and forestry; regional economic expansion; transportation; communications and labour; consumer and corporate affairs. Spending decisions were expected to be made jointly by all ministers involved with their departments in this Cabinet committee. The aim was to overcome departmental egotism and to allocate resources in the best possible way in order to achieve the aim of 'economic development'. In theory this system strengthened the element of programmatic decisions and of enlightened argument in the budgetary decision-making process.

The basic idea of the envelope system, which was slightly modified, but left in place during the Trudeau administration of 1980–4, was to set a broad framework for policies. This framework was to be controlled by the envelope (Cabinet committee) Priorities and Planning chaired by the Prime Minister. As mentioned, the day-to-day management of expenditures in the general framework set, was left to envelopes with broader job descriptions. In these envelopes different ministries were supposed to co-operate both to find the best and most efficient policy and to make optimal use of the limited resources of each envelope. However, a major conflict of interest was built into this system of budgeting, that between departmental spenders and the guardians of the public purse (Sturm 1989: 37ff.). Whenever the latter (most of the time the Prime Minister or the Finance Minister, Gillespie 1984) accepted that the logic of spending programmes deserved an exception from spending rules and expenditure limits the deficit increased. The envelope system was never intended to define an absolute ceiling of overall expenditures, but it was hoped that the kind of policy initiatives anchored in correct priorities that it generated would create sufficient economic growth to accommodate all present and future spending needs.

The harsh reality was, however, that the lack of budgetary stability in the Trudeau years soon became apparent. Neither was spending under close control, nor could the necessary efficiency gains be achieved. On the contrary, as Maslove (1984: 19f.) argues:

> Previous to PEMS a department had a limited incentive to seek out inefficient and outdated programs and to eliminate or change them. In all likelihood the money saved would stay with the department and would be available to spend on other new or expanding programs. Under PEMS, there is a greater chance that the savings will be claimed by the relevant 'envelope' and be reallocated elsewhere. And clearly, the larger the savings, the more worthwhile it is for others to fight over them. In these circumstances, the incentive for departments to examine critically their ongoing programs . . . which is never strong in the best of circumstances, is even more blunted.

Trudeau first reacted to such problems with a strengthening of the guardians in the envelope system. When John Turner succeeded Pierre Elliott Trudeau as Liberal Prime Minister in 1984 he also reorganised the powerful social and regional development envelopes.

In the early 1980s the world market prices for crude oil unexpectedly started to fall. Trudeau's plan to finance his national strategy with the income created by the sale of the country's national resources was in shambles. Short-term measures had to be found to allow the government's priorities at least to hibernate. The second budget of Finance Minister, Allan MacEachen, of November 1981 could not avoid asserting both the need for fighting inflation through a policy of high interest rates and for reducing the deficit, for example, by closing off tax loopholes. At the same time this budget increased the pressure on tax income by tax expenditures which mostly favoured Canadians with middle and higher incomes. Doern and Phidd (1992: 147) report that: 'The budget produced a political disaster in an economy sinking into depression. It was widely perceived to be one that produced neither good economic nor [good] social policy.' The June 1982 budget was intended to tackle more directly the inflation problem, although it was obvious that the deficit was difficult to ignore. Again PEMS was side-lined as an instrument of priority setting. A 'Six and Five' programme (Swimmer 1984) was announced. The idea behind this programme, so the Trudeau Government claimed, was to set an example for private sector income increases by limiting wage increases for federal employees to 6 per cent in 1982 and to 5 per cent in 1983.

The 1983 and 1984 Liberal budgets were based on the expectation of a growing Canadian economy stimulated by a Special Recovery Program, which included spending programmes for capital projects and incentives for private investment over a period of four years. The Finance Minister tried to alleviate the growing concerns over the deficit in a background paper entitled 'The Federal Deficit in Perspective', which was tabled along with the budget. The paper argued that only 20–40 per cent of the deficit was structural, i.e. would not disappear automatically when the economy recovered. But the measures introduced in the 1983 budget would, after a brief transitory period, overcome the present structural problems. Deficits of the federal government, so went another argument of the Finance Minister, must also be seen in perspective. The surpluses of provincial governments have to be taken into account for an accurate overall picture of the dimensions of the general government deficit problem (Strick 1985: 182ff.).

The deficit problem becomes a regular feature of the political agenda

Since the onset of the 1982–3 recession the deficit had increased sharply. This sharp rise was entirely attributable to federal operations, especially a shortfall of tax income, because of a wide range of tax cuts (OECD 1986: 39). Although the deficit problem was not central to the election campaign after the election victory of the Progressive-Conservatives which brought Brian Mulroney into the office of Prime Minister the new Minister of Finance, Michael Wilson, soon identified the reduction of the deficit as one of the major tasks of the new government. Ottawa, it was argued, ran out of 'real money' long ago. The Trudeau Government was in the view of the Tories spending money it did not have and was therefore contributing to growing deficits. The strategic consequence of this analysis was to opt for a policy of expenditure reductions. The broader aim of deficit control was in the view of the Mulroney Government to regain business confidence, to lower interest rates, and to increase economic growth, which meant in the end to create new jobs (Prince 1986: 14). Deficit reduction on the federal level of government was complicated by the dismantling of the previous government's National Energy Program. The Western Accord of 1985 redistributed gross energy sector revenue flows from the federal government to the provinces. But the problems of transition from the old to the new government were not the only reason why the pace of budgetary change was criticised as being too slow by business groups. The prevailing incrementalism had a lot to do with the brokerage style of the new government, who wanted to consult and to reduce confrontation in policy-making.

The basic idea of the Mulroney Government with regard to deficit control was to slow down the growth of public debt until debt growth was in line with economic growth. Annual deficits were to be reduced gradually, because there was the fear that too rapid deficit reduction might risk weakening or even reversing economic recovery. In its Agenda for Economic Renewal the federal government laid down the following strategy (OECD 1988: 34):

- to reduce the growth of the public debt to no more than that of the economy over the medium term: that is, to stabilize the debt-to-GDP ratio;
- to achieve continuing, sizeable year-over-year reductions in the deficit;
- to achieve substantial year-over-year reductions in the government's financial requirements; and
- to ensure that the greater part of the fiscal progress is achieved through effective expenditure restraint and good management.

In the 1986 budget deficit spending to stimulate the economy was definitely ruled out. The major instrument for fighting the deficit was to be expenditure cuts. These included cuts in the size of staff of public administration. A task force led by the Deputy Prime Minister Eric Nielsen developed ideas for such cuts.

The annual federal deficit was reduced from 1984–5 8.6 per cent to 4.8 per cent in the fiscal year 1988–9. Economic growth was, however, still too weak to bring about a reduction in the debt-to-GDP ratio. In the years leading to the 1988 election the Mulroney Government was eager to prove that its deficit control strategy was on track. In 1988 there was still the hope that it would be a realistic aim to stabilise general government debt at 40 per cent of GDP (OECD 1988: 44). The government's deficit control strategy was helped by a period of economic boom between 1986 and 1989 which consolidated the debt-to-GDP ratio without the need for extremely brutal expenditure cuts. With hindsight the Department of Finance (1990: 63) summarised the government strategy in the following way:

Fiscal consolidation was a pillar of the government's 1984 Agenda for Economic Renewal, and spending restraint is the cornerstone of that fiscal strategy. While the deficit is affected by total budgetary expenditures, the government can only directly control program expenditures. These expenditures account for just under three-quarters of total federal spending; the rest, public debt charges, now makes up about 28 per cent of budgetary expenditures. Public debt charges can only be reduced indirectly, by getting the deficit and hence debt down and by creating an environment with lower inflation which is necessary for significant and sustainable declines in interest rates.

Public opinion was distracted from the deficit issue in the 1988 election campaign, which was turned more or less into a referendum on the US–Canada Free Trade Agreement. Here Prime Minister Mulroney showed much more consistency than with regard to his more general neo-liberal agenda, the Agenda for Economic Renewal of November 1984, with which he had started his time in office. The February 1988 Budget projected only a small decline in the federal deficit over the next two years. This reflected the assumed impact of lower oil and grain prices, the transitional effects of Stage I of the planned tax reform, which was originally designed to be deficit neutral, and the phasing out of customs duties under the Canada–United States Free Trade Agreement (OECD 1988: 45).

In the first Mulroney years not only the priorities of budgeting changed, but also its organisation. Though PEMS continued to exist formally, power of decision-making was further concentrated in the Prime Minister's office and the Ministry of Finance. Eric Nielsen, the second man in Mulroney's Cabinet, sat in all envelope meetings and reported to Priorities and Planning. When Dan Mazankowski took over Nielsen's role in 1986 he created an Operations Committee which brought together the leading figures of the different envelopes. The Committee operated parallel to PEMS structures which were de facto robbed of their ability to make decisions.

After his re-election in 1988 Brian Mulroney's Government remained under pressure to fight the budget deficit by simultaneously increasing taxes and cutting spending. Tax increases were, however, often sporadic, and it was difficult to identify the government's tax strategy. Following a more-or-less continuous year-on-year reduction in the deficit in the years 1985 to 1988, the federal government expected to achieve a balanced budget by the mid-1990s (OECD 1995: 38). Critics argue that in this period the Mulroney Government did not do enough. Fanny S. Demers (1992: 84) summarised the general mood when she wrote: 'The current government only truly started to attack the deficit problem in 1988, instead of during the relative periods of boom that the economy enjoyed from 1983 through 1987.' In the late 1980s and early 1990s it proved to be increasingly difficult to control the deficit. Sharply rising interest payments followed by weakened economic activity, i.e. a substantial shortfall in tax receipts, increased annual deficits (OECD 1992: 34). An unforeseen challenge to budgetary stability was provided in 1991 by the costs of the Gulf War. In 1991 more than half of the growth in programme spending was accounted for by increases in unemployment insurance payments, agricultural support and defence spending related to the Gulf War (OECD 1991: 52). In January 1992 the Mulroney Government even had to announce a two-month freeze on discretionary spending and on hiring in a last effort to keep the 1991–2 deficit below the planned level.

The major source of new tax income was supposed to be a new indirect tax, the Goods and Services Tax (GST). Though it was announced as the second stage of the 1988 tax reform which – following the example of the US tax reform of 1986 – had facilitated the tax code, it was also attractive to the government, because it promised to be a prolific revenue raiser and was consistent with the government's overall deficit reduction strategy. A 9 per cent GST was introduced in 1991. What the government did not foresee was the loss of confidence its deficit-reduction policies caused in the Canadian electorate. The GST turned out to be the most unpopular tax in Canadian history (Brown-John 1994: 21). To demonstrate its resolve not to use additional income from GST for additional programme spending the government in 1991 established by law a Debt Servicing and Reduction Fund (DSRF). The DSRF was supposed to apply GST revenues as well as net privatisation proceeds and voluntary contributions to service and reduce the debt (OECD 1991: 53). One could argue, however, as Abele (1991: 18) did, that the fund was 'a cosmetic gesture', because 'once the revenue is collected, there is no way to tell

"GST Dollars" from other tax income or from foregone expenditures.' In addition, total GST revenues would have amounted to only about half of what the government had to pay annually to service the debt. So the reduction part of the Fund's title was misleading.

With regard to reform of the decision-making institutions at the level of the federal government the process of centralisation of decision-making in the PEMS was brought to its logical end. PEMS was abolished, because the conventional wisdom in the Mulroney Government was that PEMS encouraged spending (Graham 1989: 21). The new post-1988 Cabinet structure strengthened above all the guardians of the public purse and increased their numbers. It eliminated all spending powers of departmental ministers. The Operations Committee, chaired by the Deputy Prime Minister, was upgraded and formalised. It could now even act as gate-keeper for the Priorities and Planning Committee (P&P). Only after the Operations Committee's approval could Priorities and Planning exercise its role, which was to control any significant government expenditure, even if it was to be taken from existing programme reserves. Smaller routine programmes had to be approved by the Treasury Board. In addition a new Expenditure Review Committee, chaired by the Prime Minister, was established. It had the task of conducting an ongoing review of all government expenditures to ensure appropriate spending behaviour. Katherine Graham (1989: 19ff.) aptly summarised the second-term Mulroney Government's obsession with institutionalised expenditure controls:

> There are at least four bodies concerned with guarding the public purse: the Department of Finance, the Treasury Board, the Expenditure Review Committee and P&P. The Operations Committee may also have a role in dealing with spending matters. . . . The new federal decision-making system certainly has guardians, possibly so many of them that they will be tripping over each other.

In its second term the Mulroney Government also continued its policy of controlling the cost of staff working for the federal government. It operated with fixed federal wage budgets which meant that every wage increase had to be paid for by job losses. In addition, the government reduced public sector employment substantially. The 'down-sizing' of the federal bureaucracy was supposed to have a major impact on the deficit, especially when, as was the case for the 1991–2 budget, the recession led to a greater budget deficit than was originally forecast. Eugene Swimmer (1992: 285) has questioned, however, the rationale of this restraint programme by a simple comparison of the effects of this policy with the impact of changes in interest rates on the deficit:

> In 1990–91, all personnel costs (including management) made up 12 per cent of the federal budget. If these costs increased by 5 per cent as a result of free collective bargaining, the additional cost would amount to $870 million. Although this number seems large in the abstract, it must be considered in comparison to other government policy choices. The Bank of Canada's decision in 1990 to push up the Canadian short-term interest rate to 3.3 percentage points above the US rate (instead of maintaining the traditional 1.9 point differential) generated $2.5 billion in annual interest payments on the total national debt.

Table 3.2 Total federal and provincial net public debt in % of GDP

1989–90	74.7
1990–1	79.1
1991–2	86.7
1992–3	95.7
1993–4	102.0
1994–5	104.9
1995–6	106.3
1996–7	105.9
1997–8 (est.)	104.1

Source: Economics Department, Toronto Dominion Bank.

Jean Chrétien won the 1993 election on a Liberal platform which under the title 'Creating Opportunity' (the so-called Red Book) promised a balanced approach to deficit reduction. The aim was to reduce the annual deficit to 3 per cent of the GDP (the same criterion which can be found in the Maastricht treaty) by 1996. An increase in taxes was almost ruled out, because of the already higher tax burden of Canadians compared to US citizens. Also inacceptable to the new government was old-style Keynesian deficit spending. The Red Book did, however, mention expenditure cuts.

The 1994 budget defined areas of spending cuts and upheld the tight control of public sector wages. It was largely uninspiring. Observers soon compared it to the not very successful last Mulroney budgets. Though the economy recovered briefly in 1994 and the federal government financial deficit declined for the first time in five years, the federal debt as percentage of the GDP still grew to almost 75 per cent. The 1995 budget was much stricter with regard to expenditure cuts which covered not only a whole range of policy areas, but also federal–provincial transfers, and drastically reduced public sector jobs (the plan was 15 per cent). With such a budget the annual deficit could be reduced and the sharp rise of the overall federal debt was halted. The 1996 budget continued the multi-year spending cuts announced in 1995. All indicators seemed to support the expectation that the budget deficit was now under control, and that the annual deficit could be reduced. A balanced budget in the fiscal year 1999–2000 seemed possible. What remained a serious problem was the size of the net public debt total of federal and provincial governments which had surpassed the 100 per cent of GDP ratio in the 1993–4 fiscal year.

Prime Minister Chrétien did not change the centralised structure of cabinet decision-making on the budget introduced by his Progressive–Conservative predecessor. In 1995 he initiated, however, a new Expenditure Management System as an additional mechanism to control federal spending. The latter was designed to put a ceiling on spending. After ministries have received their share of the budget all new spending will have to come from internal reallocations of resources either from within or among the relevant ministries. There is no longer a contingency reserve to pay for unforeseen or extra expenditures. Planning too, once synonymous with programming, is reduced to a mechanism to control future spending. All ministries have to submit a three-year business plan which explains future departmental activities in the framework of given approved expenditure levels (OECD 1995: 64f.).

The cost and complexity of having both the unpopular GST at the federal level and various systems of retail sales taxes on the provincial level, each with different tax bases, rates, formulae for calculation, and reporting requirements, has provided a strong impetus for the Chrétien Government to look for an alternative system of taxation, which, however, should be neutral with regard to the tax income of the federal government. The federal government proposed a harmonisation of sales taxes on the federal and provincial level. Provinces with lower taxes were, however, opposed to a policy of tax increases, whereas provinces with higher taxes feared revenue losses. In 1996 only Newfoundland, Nova Scotia and New Brunswick accepted a federal proposal for a harmonised sales tax effective from April 1997, which has a common base and a single administration. The federal government in return had to agree to pay over a transitional period of four years for the tax losses which the three provinces expect.

The institutional framework for decisions on the deficit

The constitution (BNA Act, 1867) in its Article 91 gives the federal parliament (in practice the federal government) control over 'the public debt and property' and 'the borrowing of money on the public credit'. Its Article 92 also stipulates the power of the provinces with regard to 'the borrowing of money on the sole credit of the Province'.

As in Britain the budgetary process in Canada is under the control of the political executive. The central figure for giving direction to deficit control initiatives, be they institutional or policy-oriented, is the Prime Minister. He controls Parliament and his Cabinet, though for non-Liberal governments the Senate may at times turn out to be an obstacle: in 1991, for example, the Mulroney Government had to resort to an unprecedented use of additional Senate appointments to change the majority in the Upper House in order to pass legislation which installed the GST.

Some observers have even argued that Parliament has virtually no policy role – only the power to oppose, criticise and scrutinise (Doern and Phidd 1992: 27). In the Cabinet priority-setting has mostly been the task of a special Cabinet committee for priorities and planning. Expenditures are subdivided in different categories (Doern and Phidd 1992: 176):

> The 'A' budget refers to those expenditures of an ongoing nature needed to maintain existing programs or to fund them at new levels caused by population growth. The 'B' budget refers to expenditures on new initiatives or programs and is also often called the 'policy reserve'. Increasingly, the level of scarcity is such that an 'X' budget must be created, one that identifies items in the 'A' base that can or should be eliminated in whole or in part either to achieve restraint or, more typically, to be reallocated to some new 'B' budget initiative.

During the last twenty years this basic structure of the budgetary process has been overhauled to strengthen the role of the departmental minister with regard to detailed expenditure decisions and to strengthen the role of the Prime Minister as guardian of the public purse. This meant that the political sanctity of the 'A' budget was questioned, the room for new expenditures was considerably narrowed and all expenditures came under close scrutiny. In times of scarcity when deficit reduction had become one of the government priorities the style of budgeting changed, too. When bargaining is oriented towards a redistribution of growing resources it is fairly easy to avoid conflict and to engage in support for special interests. The deficit has highlighted the problem that budgeting with insufficient resources creates winners and losers in Canadian society and at the same time reduces the degree of responsibility the federal government accepts for Canada's social and regional development.

Critics of budgetary outcomes stress the importance of special interests which play a role in spending decisions independent from institutional mechanisms to control the deficit. These interests may be linked to departmental heads and to ministers, who logroll by supporting higher spending on each other's special constituencies. Robert A. Young (1991: 65) argued that the spenders in such decision-making processes are stronger than the guardians of the public purse, because the former engage in 'spending by comparison', i.e. they set expenditure limits not by considering the funds available, but by adding 'x' to funds spent on other programmes. The logical solution was to strengthen the role of the guardians in the Cabinet decision-making process, as was done by the second Mulroney Government. The appetite of special interests for greater spending could be contained. ('The special-interest pigs may still be at the trough, but none is getting much more than it used to', Young 1991: 70.)

Decision-making on deficit totals in Canada is complicated by the budgetary autonomy of the country's ten provinces. Over the last decades the latter has increased, because Canadian federalism has been moving in the direction of greater decentralisation. Provincial governments have seen this in different terms. They have often protested against the federal 'offloading' and feared that the federal government was shifting its budget problem to them.

The deficit of the consolidated government sector includes the provincial, local and hospital (PLH) sector. In terms of expenditure the PLH sector is even larger than the federal government's budget. A decisive part of the growth of sub-national spending has to do with policy fields central to the welfare state, which are under provincial responsibility, such as education, health care and social services. In the mid-1970s federal transfer payments to the provinces were reduced in order to control the federal deficit. This has influenced the budgetary balance on the provincial level. Whereas types and cost of welfare expenditures were fairly similar in all provinces, provincial income varies considerably, depending on the wealth of the province in question, its income bases, and the amounts received through transfers from the federal government. In 1995, for example, Ontario contributed 40.4 per cent to Canada's GDP and Québec 22.3 per cent. In a middle position of relative wealth were British Columbia (13.4 per cent) and Alberta 11 per cent. Poorer provinces are Manitoba with a contribution of 3.4 per cent to the Canadian GDP, Saskatchewan (3.1 per cent), Nova Scotia (2.5 per cent), New Brunswick (2 per cent), Newfoundland (1.3 per cent) and Prince Edward Island (0.3 per cent).

Table 3.3 General government and PLH budget balance (in % of GDP)

	General government annual deficit	Provincial, Local and Hospital sector (PLH) deficit
1960	1.7	1.1
1970	+0.8	0.8
1975	n.d.	1.4
1980	2.8	0.3
1981	n.d.	0.4
1982	5.9	1.5
1983	6.9	1.5
1984	6.5	0.5
1985	7.0	1.0
1986	4.8	1.4
1987	4.2	0.7
1988	2.6	+0.3
1989	3.0	0.1
1990	4.2	0.7
1991	6.3	1.9
1992	7.1	2.9
1993	7.3	2.2
1994	5.3	1.2
1995	4	
1996	3	
1997	2 (estimated)	

Sources: OECD Economic Surveys. *Financial Times,* 10.10.96: 6.

The worsening in the provinces' fiscal position was the decisive factor behind the increase in the general government deficit in the late 1980s and the early 1990s. In 1989–90 the budget deficit on the provincial level was 0.7 per cent of provincial GDP in 1992–3 it had reached 3.6 per cent (OECD 1993: 36). Since 1992 the provincial budget situation has begun to improve with fairly impressive results, though the two largest provinces, Ontario and Québec, are lagging behind. They aim at a balanced budget in the fiscal year 2000–1 and 1999–2000 respectively. By 1995–6, six of the ten provinces had balanced their budgets. In 1996–7 Alberta, Manitoba, Saskatchewan and New Brunswick had moved into significant fiscal surplus positions (OECD 1997: 35). Most provinces have now had a parliamentary vote in favour of a balanced budget. Their methods of controlling the deficit are surprisingly diverse, as the OECD (1997: 37) reports:

> ranging from New Brunswick's four-year cumulative balanced budget requirement to Manitoba's annual balanced budget requirement that also includes non-compliance penalties through ministerial salary cuts (of up to 40 per cent). In the Yukon territory there is an election trigger if any debt is accumulated. Several jurisdictions have legislated debt repayment plans. In general, these require the reduction or elimination of debt over an extended period of time. . . . British Columbia's Financial Management Plan does not schedule any specific paydowns of debt but incorporated targets for a reduction in the debt-to-GDP ratio. Finally, in a number of provinces a referendum is required to decide on major tax increases.

These decisions were made under the pressure of financial markets which rate the provinces according to their economic performance. This has consequences with regard to the differences between interest rates on federal and provincial bonds. The greater a province's relative indebtedness, the lower the interest rates for its bonds will be.

The debt crisis in perspective

In 1984, when the C.D. Howe Institute, a Canadian think tank, presented a study on the deficit (Bruce and Purvis 1984: V), it was still necessary to explain why this issue should be dealt with at all. In the foreword to the study, one finds the statement that 'For most Canadians, who are more concerned with persistent high unemployment, action to reduce the federal deficit may appear untimely, even ill-advised.' And another C.D. Howe study of the same year (Carmichael 1984: 2ff.) stated that 'The hard fact about Canada's deficit is that for over 10 years Canadians have accepted more in services and transfers from the federal government than they have been willing to pay for.' This lack of awareness of the importance of the deficit problem was reflected in opinion polls, in which in no year more than 2 per cent of those polled indicated that they believed the deficit or the national debt constituted the most important economic problem facing Canada. In addition, the Mulroney Government was at first perceived as being unwilling to tackle tough issues such as reducing the federal deficit (Prince 1986: 3).

Perceptions changed and by 1988 the deficit came to dominate the agenda of budgetary policy-making. But explanations for the deficit were not uniform, and there was no social consensus on deficit control strategies. Wolfe (1985: 133ff.) even argues that the financial and business communities were successful in exploiting the debate on the deficit to strengthen their political influence. For business interests deficits were caused above all by the combined result of uncontrolled spending on social programmes and of inefficient and interventionist bureaucracies. Labour unions and consumer groups pointed to the need for an increase in tax income, especially by taxes on corporations and upper-income earners (Doern, Maslove and Prince 1988: 206).

The Progressive–Conservative Government of Brian Mulroney stressed from start that the economy was in disequilibrium in two areas: unemployment and the deficit. The government did not see the need for a policy choice, but argued that its medium-term approach was to emphasise the importance of sound public-sector finances as a precondition for sustainable growth in the longer run (OECD 1986: 20).

What above all dramatised the situation was the speed with which the deficit situation deteriorated. The total debt-to-GDP ratio rose from roughly 27 per cent in 1980 to 75 per cent in 1995 and by 1995 every fourth tax dollar had to be used only to pay the annual interest on the accumulated debt. Canada's relative position among the major OECD economies had also dramatically worsened: Canada went from having the second lowest net debt-to-GDP ratio amongst the G7 economies in 1980 to having the second highest (after Italy) in 1994 (OECD 1995: 47). Debt levels were close to OECD average in the early 1980s, but in the early 1990s they exceeded the OECD average by more than 20 percentage points (OECD 1993: 41).

In contrast to Germany and Britain, Canada financed its debt to a great extent externally. At the beginning of the 1990s almost a quarter of the public debt had been financed by foreign investors (a phenomenon of special importance for the provincial level), whereas at the beginning of the 1980s the corresponding share was one-tenth (OECD 1993: 41). The ratio of net external liabilities to GDP for Canada was 45.5 per cent of GDP in 1994. The OECD in its 1995 report (p. 53) warned that the magnitude of this debt, together with the burden of debt service it places on the current account, may lead to a greater volatility in the exchange rate of the Canadian Dollar. Another consequence may be financial 'crowding out' of industrial investors,[4] if interest rate increases are required in order to attract the necessary domestic and foreign savings.

The argument was also made that deficits, and especially deficit-control policies, may threaten the Canadian federation. With the cut-back of transfer payments to the provinces Ottawa has, at least temporarily, lost the ability to use central government funds for providing leadership in policy-making. If the central government cuts deeply enough to provoke a substantial increase of the relative importance of provincial taxation, it will end up as a considerably less important force in the Canadian economy (Doern and Purchase 1991: 16f.).

Today debt reduction policies are fairly popular in Canada. Opinion polls suggest that about 40 per cent of Canadians are willing to forgo tax cuts and new spending initiatives in order to tackle the debt (*Financial Times*, 24.2.98, p. 7).

Deficit control policies

There are no constitutional limits on federal and provincial borrowing powers in Canada. Both levels of government may borrow from both within and outside the country. One principle of deficit control policies in Canada was to choose a strategy which implied a moderate pace of deficit reduction, gradually building up over time. For Canada deficit control meant both higher taxes and radical expenditure cuts. Whereas neo-conservatives in the United States in the first term of the Reagan administration believed that reduced taxes would stimulate the economy in a way that created higher tax income, in turn allowing higher defence spending and reduction of the deficit,[5] the Canadian Tories led by Brian Mulroney argued that moderate tax increases were justified to restore fiscal stability and to restore the revenue yield (in percentage of GDP) of earlier decades. Taxation was not the major instrument for deficit control.

Spending cuts represented 98 per cent of the deficit reduction achieved in 1985–6, then 67 per cent in 1986–7 and 70 per cent in 1990–1 (Prince 1986: 49). In the 1995 budget the spending cuts still outweighed revenue increases by a ratio of 7 to 1. Deficit reductions between late 1993 and late 1997 were to about 90 per cent due to expenditure cuts (OECD 1997: 35). This is not surprising. As a general rule expenditure cuts were much preferred to increases in taxation for two reasons, which have both to do with the geographic location of Canada next to the United States. On the one hand it was important to maintain tax levels which would continue to attract the necessary US investments to Canada. On the other hand Canadian citizens compare their tax burden with that of their neighbours south of the border, thus defining what they find acceptable.

Expenditure cuts affected above all civil service salary, public investment and social and defence expenditures. In the early 1990s the reduction of the size of the civil service was accompanied by government reorganisation and privatisations. More than fifty agencies and other government entities were eliminated or consolidated. Since the mid-1980s forty Crown corporations (public enterprises) have been privatised, which meant a reduction of public employment of about 100,000 (OECD 1994: 59). Public service bashing developed into a kind of traditional government practice since the 1970s (see for example: Zussman 1986). Following the line of argument of the Trudeau and Mulroney Governments the Chrétien Government, too, attacked the waste in the federal bureaucracy. Reduced federal programmes meant reduced federal employment. In the three years from 1994–5 to 1997–8 Prime Minister Chrétien reduced the number of federal employees by about 15 per cent (i.e. 55,000 jobs). Another area of substantive cuts has been defence. Cuts included the closure of military bases at home and abroad. With respect to the cuts in overseas aid it has to be mentioned that the size of Canadian programmes for this purpose was in the past well above the OECD average, and that measured by this yardstick spending patterns in Canada are only getting more similar to those of other western democracies.

Another recurrent feature of deficit control policies in Canada is the reduction of the role of the federal government as provider of public goods and public services and a strengthening of the role of the provinces. Canadian federalism has steadily increased the relative autonomy of the provinces in financial matters. Shared responsibility of the federal government and the provinces has been transformed into the model of an annual one-time limited federal grant with additional funds provided by the provinces depending on their own decisions. In this way the federal government gains complete control of the financial totals transferred to the provinces and avoids the danger of unforeseen spending, because of legal obligations to support special government programmes. Since 1990 the size of per capita transfers for the Established Programs Financing (EPF) had been frozen in nominal terms, which meant, taking account of inflation, a de facto cut. The EPF was the largest transfer programme accounting for 58 per cent of transfers to the provinces in 1994–5.

The Canada Assistance Plan (CAP), which made up 22 per cent of transfers to the provinces in 1994–5, was capped by the federal government for the three highest-income provinces (Alberta, British Columbia and Ontario) by an imposition of an annual limit of 5 per cent for its growth. The right of the federal government to impose this ceiling was upheld by a decision of the Supreme Court in August 1991. In April 1996 transfers under the CAP, with funding of provincial social welfare programmes based on a shared-cost basis, were merged into a block grant with those transfers of the EPF system, which used to provide block grants to

Table 3.4 Federal-provincial transfers (% GDP)

	1985	1993/94	1994/95
Canada Assistance Plan	0.8	1.1	1.1
Established Programs Financing	1.3	3.0	2.9
Equalisation	–	1.1	1.1
TOTAL MAJOR TRANSFERS	–	5.2	5.1

Source: OECD 1995: 142.

finance provincial post-secondary education and health (OECD 1995: 41). The new block grant is called Canada Health and Social Transfer (CHST). The federal government plans to reduce the block grant for the CHST from 5 per cent of GDP in 1995–6 to 4 per cent in 1998–9. In addition to EPF and CAP there are equalisation payments, which accounted for 23 per cent of total transfers to the provinces in 1994–5. These payments compensate the provinces for differences in their ability to raise revenue.

Probably there is a political and an economic limit to deficit control policies which concentrate on the reduction of transfer payments to the provinces. A political limit could be seen in the danger to the cohesion of the Canadian federation which may result from a further reduction of common interests and involvement of federal and provincial governments. An economic problem may arise if federal cutbacks seriously jeopardise the provincial deficit control policies.

In contrast to the deficit control strategy of the British Government the Canadian Government did not at first rely on privatisation proceeds to balance the budget. To use privatisations as a serious income earner for the federal government would have been difficult, anyhow, because in Canada the state sector in industry which could be privatised was much smaller than its British equivalent. In addition, the privatisation policy which started in the mid-1980s was implemented relatively cautiously, and often restricted by competing aims of government policies, such as social and regional development. So the budgetary impact of privatisation initiatives was limited. It was estimated that in the mid-1980s the total value of the Crowns (i.e. the nationalised industries) was 60 billion dollars. Until 1992 only 3.6 billion dollars were added to federal income by 24 privatisations (Stanbury 1994: 218).

Prime Minister Brian Mulroney tried unsuccessfully to control the deficit by legislation. In 1989 an Expenditure Review Committee of the Cabinet was installed. In 1990 the Mulroney Government introduced the Expenditure Control Act which reduced, froze or limited spending in every policy field except major transfers to households and equalisation payments to some provinces. The ambitious aim of the Act was to reduce the deficit to GDP ratio to 1 per cent by 1994. In 1992 a Spending Control Act followed, which limited programme spending till 1995–6 (when the Act was not renewed by the Chrétien Government) to the levels projected in the 1991 budget. Any overspending in one year had to be recovered in the following two years. On the revenue side the Act increased unemployment insurance premiums to compensate for the rising costs of unemployment (OECD 1993:

32). The problem, which legislation to control expenditures could not solve, was the unexpected weakness in the growth of revenues, which would have necessitated even greater cuts if new deficits were to be avoided. Deficit control legislation may, however, have a political rationale. Legislation may be useful to convince the markets that a government's intention to control expenditures will be implemented, and it may force the opposition to explain to the public where it stands with regard to politically painful cuts (Doern and Phidd 1992: 186).

The 1995 budget savings of the Chrétien Government were based on the results of a major 'Programme Review' which closely considered which programmes and services the federal government should be providing, and argued about the most effective and cost-efficient way of doing so. To undertake this review government ministers were asked to apply six tests to their programmes and services. They had to check:

- the extent to which their programmes and services serve the public interest;
- the necessity of government involvement (as opposed to the private sector);
- the appropriateness of the federal role (as opposed to other levels of government);
- the scope for public sector/private sector partnerships;
- the scope for increased efficiency, and
- affordability (OECD 1995: 63f.).

The result of the Programme Review was that the government developed a strategy for savings to reduce the budget deficit which included (OECD 1995: 64) first of all the elimination or at least a substantial reduction of all kinds of subsidies. Business subsidies, for example, were to be reduced by 60 per cent by 1997–8. The largest savings were expected from the elimination of the subsidy to the rail transportation of prairie grain. A second aspect of the government strategy was the redesign of programmes to make them more efficient and cost-effective. Regional development agencies, for example, were no longer to be involved in the provision of grants and subsidies. It was planned that they should instead act as regional delivery offices for federal programmes. More efficiency was also expected from the merger and consolidation of government programmes. For instance, operations and equipment were to be integrated among some departments and various labour market programmes were to be rationalised under one umbrella. A third new idea the government introduced was the devolution of programmes or activities to other levels of government, such as the management of freshwater habitat which was to be transferred to provinces, and that of airports which was to be shifted to local authorities. Finally, the government aimed at the commercialisation or privatisation of activities, in particular, the sale of the remaining government interest in Petro-Canada, the privatisation of Canadian National (railways) and the commercialisation of Transport Canada's Air Navigation System.

In September 1995 the federal government reduced its ownership of Petro-Canada from 70 to 20 per cent, in November of the same year Canadian National was sold, and in December the government announced an agreement to sell the national air traffic control network to Nav Canada, a non-profit organisation.

A new device with regard to deficit control policies was the use of deliberately unambitious financial planning, the inclusion of so-called 'prudence factors'. Finance Minister, Paul Martin, set rolling targets for the deficit for only two years in the future. He based these targets on very pessimistic assumptions about the growth of the GDP and the development of interest rates. In addition deficit targets also included a contingency reserve which could not be spent elsewhere and had therefore only the purpose of keeping the deficit on target. Since 1995 actual deficits have tended to be even below the Finance Minister's targets (Courchene 1997: 40).

Deficits – the Canadian experience

Though in Canada both the politicians and the general public were late to acknowledge that the deficit was a problem, Canada demonstrated how fast a country's budgetary problems can be turned around. General government finances have moved from a deficit of 5.9 per cent of GDP in 1994 to Canada's first balanced budget in almost 30 years 1998–9. Today discussions have begun on what do with the emerging budget surpluses. Prime Minister Chrétien has indicated that half of future surpluses over the course of his four-year mandate will go towards new spending initiatives and the remainder will be used to cover tax cuts and reduce Canada's debt (*Financial Times*, 24.2.98, p. 7).

In the 1980s even the Conservative Mulroney Government seemed unable to distance itself clearly from past spending practices. The deficit in the first Mulroney years remained what it had been under Trudeau, a dependent variable, dependent on both the success of the government's macro-economic policies (which at a later stage included the Free Trade Agreement with the United States) and its efforts to control expenditures by a constant reorganisation of cabinet decision-making.

Not until the 1990s did the deficit become the central topic of federal and provincial budgeting on which all political fire-power was concentrated. The political decision on the federal level radically to cut public expenditures, including a substantial reduction of government personnel and the reduction of transfers to other levels of government, and higher than expected tax income consolidated the budget. Social redistribution which negatively affects the poorer strata of the society and a further decentralisation of Canadian federalism were the immediate consequences of this strategy.

Capital markets, which are extremely important for the financing of provincial budgets, reacted very positively to deficit reduction policies, which first led to balanced budgets on the provincial level. Canada now needs to borrow little new money, and if she temporarily has to do so, it is possible to negotiate comparatively low interest rates. This does not mean, however, that for Canada the debt problem is solved. Canada's net public debt-to-GDP ratio is still the third highest of all OECD countries (1996: 70.3 per cent). Now that the deficit is under control the federal government has gained greater flexibility with regard to its spending priorities, but it seems to be unavoidable that the reduction or even elimination of public debt remains on the political agenda.

Typical for the Canadian experience is the fact that efficient strategies to fight the budget deficit were dependent upon a reorganisation of cabinet decision-making. The decisions on the necessary expenditure cuts could not be made in the old context of cabinet committees (envelopes) who were given a broad task, such as social or economic development of the nation, and which were expected to hammer out compromises between the ministries involved on how to best achieve these aims. The 'envelopes' only produced demands for greater spending, and single ministries even claimed additional 'emergencies' outside the policy and expenditure management system (PEMS). The Prime Ministers of the last two decades agreed that what was needed was a strengthened role for the guardians of the public purse. In a parliamentary democracy the strength of the guardians is critically dependent on the Prime Minister's support. As a consequence Cabinet decision-making was centralised to a degree which in Britain with a similar political system may be the rule, but which for Canada meant a weakening of the role of Cabinet ministers. The centralisation of spending decisions was politically facilitated by developments in Canada's federalism. The central government in Ottawa was not too unhappy to give in to demands of the provinces, especially of Québec and of Canada's western provinces, for further decentralisation of tax and spending decisions. In this way Ottawa could reduce the pressure on its meagre finances. For Cabinet this means that it has now less to decide on and that there are fewer occasions in which centralised decision-making in Cabinet can lead to inner-Cabinet conflict.

Notes

1. In greater detail see Sturm 1989.
2. It is often forgotten to add: 'in a fully employed economy'. One should also mention that the empirical proof for crowding out is difficult, and that it is debatable whether the crowding-out hypothesis was valid for the Canadian economy.
3. This has been christened in the Canadian debate the 'declining revenue' thesis.
4. In the Canadian case increased public sector demand for credit can be accommodated by US capital inflows without curtailing credit availability to the private sector. Under these circumstances, crowding out will tend to operate – at least in the first instance – through the impact of an exchange rate appreciation on trade flows (lower exports and higher imports) rather than through lower investment (OECD 1986: 44).
5. 'The bottom line was that the whole thing had to balance. We couldn't have a deficit – not in those days' (Stockman 1986: 62f.).

References

Abele, Frances (1991) 'The politics of fragmentation', in: Abele, Frances (ed.), *How Ottawa Spends. 1991–91: The Politics of Fragmentation*, Ottawa: Carleton UP, pp. 1–32.

Bakker, Isabella (1990) 'The size and scope of government: Robin Hood sent packing?', in: Whittington, Michael S. and Williams, Glen (eds), *Canadian Politics in the 1990s*, 3rd edition, Scarborough (Ont.): Nelson Canada, pp. 423–47.

Bird, Richard M. (1979) *Financing Canadian Government: A Quantitative Overview*, Toronto: Canadian Tax Foundation.

Brown-John, Lloyd (1994) *The Great Canadian Constitutional Referendum Debate/Morass, 1990–1992*, Leicester: Centre for Federal Studies.

Bruce, Neil and Purvis, Douglas D. (1984) *Evaluating the Deficit. The Case for Budget Cuts*, Toronto: C.D. Howe Institute.

Butler, Dan and Macnaughton, Bruce D. (1984) 'More of less for whom? Debating directions for the public sector', in: Whittington, Michael S. and Williams, Glen (eds), *Canadian Politics in the 1980s*, Toronto: Methuen, pp. 1–32.

Carmichael, Edward A. (1984) *Tackling the Federal Deficit*, Toronto: C.D. Howe Institute.

Courchene, Thomas J. (1997) 'Subnational Budgetary and Stabilization Policies in Canada and Australia', Paper presented at the ZEI-NBER Conference on 'Budgeting Institutions and Fiscal Performance', Bonn.

Demers, Fanny S. (1992) 'The Department of Finance and the Bank of Canada: the fiscal and monetary policy mix', in: Abele, Frances (ed.), *How Ottawa Spends. 1992–93: The Politics of Competitiveness*, Ottawa: Carleton UP, pp. 79–124.

Department of Finance (1990) *The Budget*, Ottawa.

Doern, Bruce G., Maslove, Allan M. and Prince, Michael J. (1988) *Public Budgeting in Canada*, Ottawa: Carleton UP.

Doern, Bruce G. and Phidd, Richard W. (1992) *Canadian Public Policy. Ideas, Structure, Process*, 2nd edition, Scarborough (Ont.): Nelson Canada.

Doern, Bruce G. and Purchase, Bryne B. (1991) 'Whither Ottawa?', in: Doern, Bruce G. and Purchase, Bryne B. (eds), *Canada at Risk? Canadian Public Policy in the 1990s*, Toronto/ Calgary, pp. 1–21.

Donner, Arthur W. and Peters, Douglas D. (1979) *The Monetarist Counter-Revolution. A Critique of Canadian Monetary Policy 1975–1979*, Toronto: James Lorimer.

Gillespie, W. Irwin (1984) 'The Department of Finance and PEMS: increased influence or reduced monopoly power?', in: Maslove, Allan M. (ed.) *How Ottawa Spends. 1984: The New Agenda*, Toronto: Methuen, pp. 189–214.

Graham, Katherine A. (1989) 'Discretion and the governance of Canada', in: Graham, Katherine A. (ed.), *How Ottawa Spends. 1989–90: The Buck Stops Where?*, Ottawa: Carleton UP, pp. 1–24.

Maslove, Allan M. (1984) 'Ottawa's new agenda: the issues and constraints', in: Maslove, Allan M. (ed.), *How Ottawa Spends. 1984. The New Agenda*, Toronto: Methuen, pp. 1–30.

OECD (1986) *Economic Surveys (Canada)*, Paris: OECD.

OECD (1988) *Economic Surveys (Canada)*, Paris: OECD.

OECD (1991) *Economic Surveys (Canada)*, Paris: OECD.

OECD (1992) *Economic Surveys (Canada)*, Paris: OECD.

OECD (1993) *Economic Surveys (Canada)*, Paris: OECD.

OECD (1994) *Economic Surveys (Canada)*, Paris: OECD.

OECD (1995) *Economic Surveys (Canada)*, Paris: OECD.

OECD (1996) *Economic Surveys (Canada)*, Paris: OECD.

OECD (1997) *Economic Surveys (Canada)*, Paris: OECD.

Prince, Michael J. (1986) 'The Mulroney agenda: a right turn for Ottawa?', in: Prince, Michael J. (ed.), *How Ottawa Spends. 1986–87: Tracking the Tories*, Toronto: Methuen, pp. 1–60.

Savoie, Donald J. (1990) 'Thé politics of public spending in Canada, governments in Canada: an empirical study, in: Bernier, Robert and Gow, James Iain (eds), *Un état réduit? A Down-sized State*, Sainte-Foy (Québec): Presse de l'Université du Quebec, pp. 165–219.

Schneider, Steffen (1997) 'Von der neoliberalen Agenda zur Fourth National Policy? Entwicklungslinien kanadischer Wirtschaftspolitik in den 80er und 90er Jahren', in: Schultze, Rainer-Olaf and Schneider, Steffen (eds), *Kanada in der Krise. Analysen zum Verfassungs-, Wirtschafts- und Parteiensystemwandel in den 80er und 90er Jahren*, Bochum: Brockmeyer, pp. 123–163.

Stanbury, William T. (1994) *Privatization by Federal and Provincial Governments in Canada*, Toronto, Buffalo, London: University of Toronto Press.

Stockman, David A. (1986) *The Triumph of Politics*, London: Bodley Head.

Strick, John C. (1985) *Canadian Public Finance*. 3rd edition, Toronto: Holt, Rinehart and Winston.

Sturm, Roland (1989) *Haushaltspolitik in westlichen Demokratien*, Baden-Baden: Nomos.

Swimmer, Eugene (1984) 'Six and five', in: Maslove, Allan M. (ed.), *How Ottawa Spends. 1984: The New Agenda*, Toronto: Methuen, pp. 240–81.

Swimmer, Eugene with Kinaschuk, Kjerstine (1992) 'Staff relations under the Conservative Government: the Singers change but the song remains the same', in: Abele, Frances (ed.), *How Ottawa Spends. 1992–93: The Politics of Competitiveness*, Ottawa: Carleton UP, pp. 267–312.

Wolfe, David A. (1985) 'The Politics of the Deficit', in: Doern, Bruce G. (Research Coordinator), *The Politics of Economic Policy*, Toronto/Buffalo/London: University of Toronto Press, pp. 111–62.

Young, Robert A. (1991) 'Effecting change: do we have the political system to get us where we want to go?', in: Doern, Bruce G. and Purchase, Bryne B. (eds), *Canada at Risk? Canadian Public Policy in the 1990s*, Toronto and Calgary: C.D. Howe, pp. 59–80.

Zussman, David (1986) 'Walking the tightrope: the Mulroney Government and the public service', in: Prince, Michael J. (ed.), *How Ottawa Spends. 1986–87: Tracking the Tories*, Toronto: Methuen, pp. 250–82.

Chapter 4

Germany

The history of the deficit problem[1]

The deficit finds acceptance: from the post-war reconstruction period to the Grand Coalition

Post-war (West) Germany was in the privileged position of a fresh start both with regard to its economic constitution and with regard to the more general guidelines which were to define the framework of 'good government' and prudent financial strategies. In addition, historical circumstances ensured a very advantageous state for the country's public finances. The currency reform of 1948, which introduced the DM, eliminated most of West Germany's internal debt. Foreign debt, which had plagued the German Reich after the First World War and had led to economic and political instability in the Weimar Republic, was a relatively minor problem in post-war Germany.

The victorious powers of the First World War had insisted on large-scale reparation payments, which became one of the major causes for the economic problems of the Weimar Republic. After the Second World War the Western Allied Powers did not repeat this mistake and found a compromise for West Germany's debt repayments. This compromise did not strangle the country's economy. Except for payments to Israel no kind of reparation payments were expected from West Germany. A settlement for the repayment of post-war aid was soon found. The London agreement on German foreign debt of 27 February 1953 laid down the procedures for the repayment of Germany's pre-war debt and fixed its amount. Germany's pre-war debt was calculated to be 13.7 billion DM. In the first few years West Germany had to pay back an annual amount of 550 million DM and later of 750 million DM. In the mid-1980s the total amount of Germany's pre-war debt had been repaid (Abelshauser 1983: 17).

Other factors also contributed to West Germany's low debt. The country's constitutional consensus echoed a cautious public attitude towards the deficit financing of public policies. The then Article 115 of the Basic Law (the German constitution) stipulated that only under exceptional circumstances were deficits permissible. This budgetary consensus was based on the general notion of the virtues of a balanced budget. The quality of budgetary policies was measured by the amount of financial surplus it produced. Deficits were regarded as an indicator of political mismanagement.

In the 1950s it was not very difficult for politicians to respect this general orientation of budgetary policies. The economic boom period which followed the Korean War stimulated the West German economy and created tax income for the government. In addition, domestic consumption financed by the relative economic success of the German post-war economy ('the economic miracle') grew rapidly and contributed to sustained economic growth. As a legacy of the legislation of the Allied Powers tax levels at first remained relatively high, a factor which was also responsible for the very good shape West Germany's public finances were in in the 1950s. By 1953 the federal government's budget was in surplus,[2] and by 1955 the Finance Minister had amassed a treasury of five billion DM.

There were important arguments at the time in favour of a prudent strategy for spending this surplus, above all with regard to possible negative economic side-effects. High taxes had helped the government to control inflation, but overspending could perhaps endanger the newly won economic stability. Chancellor Adenauer saw, however, in his government's budget surplus a convenient tool for maximising his re-election prospects. In the pre-1957 general election period chunks of the surplus were used, for example, to finance new social policies, especially a very costly pension reform. This reform indexed pensions so that their levels increased parallel to the rise of the average gross income of German workers and employees.

The decision to use budget surpluses for the handing out of economic favours to special interests and/or groups in society who successfully lobbied the government was in some respect a landmark decision. It created a precedent, because it invited pressure groups into the arena of budgetary decision-making, an arena which until then had been regarded as the prerogative of government. It is important to stress this fact in a comparative context. Contrary to the traditions of Anglo-Saxon democracies, German post-war democracy had started on the assumption that the spheres of society and of the state could be neatly separated. In this context it seemed to be inappropriate to lobby for special interests. Interest groups had to wait and see what budgetary policies the government thought to be appropriate. This decision therefore also legitimised to a certain extent clientelism and pre-election spending sprees. The dilemma which arose from the fact that the political belief in an ever booming economy (Lutz 1984) created expectations in society of continuing government largesse seemed to be an obvious one. It was not difficult to predict that in the foreseeable future there would be a limit to the growth of income for the government, which would not be matched by a limit to the financial wishes of countless group interests. Though in the late 1950s the economy still went from success to success some politicians, among them the Economics Minister Ludwig Erhard, were worried about the political consequences of policies which disregarded financial prudence. Erhard criticised the undemocratic nature of influence by non-elected representatives of interest groups and the beginnings of what he feared would result in a new form of government, namely government by pressure groups with devastating budgetary consequences.

In 1962 the new spending policies created a deficit for the federal budget for the first time since 1953 (Möller and Schwebler n.d.: 222ff.). In 1963 net government borrowing more than trebled. It was temporarily reduced by changes in the pattern of distribution of tax income between the federal government and the states (*Länder*) in favour of the former. Tax reductions in 1964 and the pre-election budget of 1965 again increased considerably the annual net government borrowing. In the economic environment of the West Germany of the early 1960s what would today be a minor change created the impression of an explosion of the public debt. In the period between late 1957 and late 1963 the federal debt had already grown from 22 billion DM to 35.5 billion DM. From 1963 to 1966 it grew by another 7.2 billion DM (*Deutsche Bundesbank* data, *Bundestagsdrucksache* 11/8472, p. 379).

In the aftermath of the 1965 election the re-elected Chancellor Erhard (who had been in office since 1963) found himself in an awkward and unusual situation. For the first time in West Germany's post-war history the economy showed signs of weakness. The recession robbed the federal budget of tax income. This happened in a situation in which increases of federal income would have been needed to finance the new expenditure policies promised to the voters by Erhard in the run-up to the 1965 election. Chancellor Erhard reacted to the economic challenge in the traditional manner of a politician who had always defended the principles of the post-war budgetary consensus. He accepted the idea that whenever a government is confronted with reduced levels of income, it has either to raise taxes or to reduce spending, or it has to do both to make up for the shortage of resources. Erhard favoured a strategy which combined budgetary instruments. He introduced legislation to reduce spending on social programmes, some of which had been initiated by himself in his pre-election campaign, and he tried to convince his Liberal coalition partner to accept tax increases. His tax policies failed, however. The Liberals were not prepared to support tax increases and left Erhard's Government, not least to demonstrate their strength and independence. The major reason for the lack of flexibility of the Liberals in budgetary matters were non-financial ones. The Liberals had to prove to the German voter that they were able to fulfill electoral promises. In the past they had deeply disappointed their voters, because in 1961 they had campaigned against a new chancellorship of Konrad Adenauer, but then agreed after the election to join a coalition which Adenauer was to lead until 1963.

A new coalition government of Socialdemocrats and Christian Democrats replacing the post-war coalition of Liberals and Christian Democrats took over in 1966. The Socialdemocrats and the Christian Democrats formed the so-called 'Grand Coalition', which had a two-thirds majority in Parliament (*Bundestag*) and in the Second Chamber (*Bundesrat*). This meant that the new coalition controlled a majority strong enough to change the German constitution. What proved to be decisive for the future course of public spending in Germany was not only the fact that the party political composition of government changed in 1966, but also that in 1966 a new economic philosophy was enthroned. The idea that the central purpose of budgeting should be to secure balanced budgets (and if possible a surplus), was now regarded as obsolete. The Grand Coalition wanted to 'modernise' its economic policies, and it used its parliamentary strength to change the constitution and the laws on budgeting accordingly. The government saw Germany lagging behind world-wide and in comparison to its European neighbours, because it still had not applied the lessons of Keynesianism to its budgetary policy-making process.

German economists now argued that what Chancellor Erhard did during the 1965–6 economic crisis, namely to reduce public spending in order to make up for the reduction of tax income, had been a recipe for disaster, because the government's spending restraint deepened the country's economic crisis. During an economic crisis, when private investments are reduced the worst thing a government can do, so it was argued, is to reduce public investments simultaneously. This only magnifies the economic problem of underinvestment and creates additional unemployment. The leading politicians of the Grand Coalition decided to avoid such a negative role for the state in the event of any future economic crisis. Budgetary strategies were formulated into law which were intended to make up for the deficiencies of the business cycle. In a future recession the plan was to increase public investment, if necessary by deficit financed spending, in order to restart the economy. An increase in the public debt caused by this strategy was seen as being unproblematic, because the debt could be reduced when the economy was booming again. For it was assumed that when the economy had recovered from recession, it would eventually enter into a period of economic prosperity with great inflationary pressures. Efforts to control inflation would provoke tax increases. The proceeds from income generated by these anti-inflationary policies could be used for paying back the public debt incurred by earlier decisions to finance investments in a period of economic recession.

To enable the Grand Coalition and future German governments to exercise this broad control of the business cycle Article 115 of the Basic Law had to be changed. Instead of allowing deficits only under exceptional circumstances, as the old Article 115 did, the new Article 115 permitted deficit spending whenever the government believed the economy was out of balance. Balance was defined in a special law, the stability law (*Stabilitätsgesetz*) of 1967. According to this law the government is expected to intervene into the economy whenever there is a threat either to full employment, to price stability, to economic growth, or to the balance of payments. In order to rule out using public credit to increase the level of social consumption, the new article was made to stipulate that the credit level allowed in budget laws should never exceed the level of public investments. But at the same time Article 115 contained strategic advice for ignoring this restriction on excessive borrowing. It says that the restriction on borrowing is not applicable to a situation of economic imbalance as described in the stability law.

In other words the budget reforms of the 1960s gave policy-makers a free hand with regard to public spending and especially with regard to the definition of circumstances under which deficits were permissible to further the common good. It was obvious that in the real world a situation in which all four aims of the stability law were met would never occur. Even the years of Germany's economic miracle with full employment, price stability and high economic growth were unsuccessful in one respect: the balancing of exports and imports. The economic miracle could only occur because of an export boom in favour of Germany's industry. So since the mid-1960s German politicians could in practice decide for themselves whether or not they wanted to see the national economy in a 'crisis' which called for state intervention and deficit-financed spending. The federal government's freedom of action was increased furthermore by the fact that there was and indeed there is no international consensus on the exact definition of the central categories of the stability law, such as full employment (does this, for example, mean 1 per cent, 2 per cent or even 5 per cent of the population are still unemployed?). Not only did 'economic stability' remain a category which could be interpreted widely by interested parties, the term 'investments' which was supposed to limit spending under non-crisis conditions of budgetary decision-making also remained a fuzzy concept. There is no hard and fast definition for it in the budget papers or the law on budgeting.

In the late 1960s the Economics Minister of the Grand Coalition, Karl Schiller, a Socialdemocrat, and its Finance Minister, Franz Josef Strauß, a Conservative, even went so far to criticise publicly the size of the German deficit as being too small for a modern economy. They regarded deficits as a kind of engine for economic growth. In their view it was not only acceptable, but necessary that in a growing economy the deficit grew annually, too. Schiller and Strauß argued that fiscal conservatives who advocated balanced budgets had not understood that the full potential of an economy could only be mobilised by public spending at levels which corresponded to economic growth. Were governments to opt, for example, for higher taxes to finance public investments in infrastructure they would rob firms of the opportunity to invest, and they would reduce the ability of private households to accumulate wealth.

In addition to this general prejudice in favour of deficits nurtured by the Grand Coalition the growth of public deficits in the 1960s and 1970s was caused by the quest of politicians for personal electoral success. In the final analysis the latter aim proved to be more important than the strict adherence to abstract principles of financial prudence and to the logic of the Keynesian model of economic intervention the Grand Coalition had preached and popularised. Policy-makers felt justified in overspending, partly because Germany's debt level still remained far below the OECD average. Till the 1970s such a humble level of public debt was seen by West Germany's Economics Ministers as being inadequately low for a 'modern' economy. Though it was tempting for the government to give absolute priority to expenditure policies, the logic of the Keynesian management of the budget cycle was not completely ignored. The deficit-financed increase in public spending in connection with an already booming economy in the late 1960s produced inflationary pressures. The Grand Coalition reacted in 1969 to these pressures and limited the amount of the deficit in that budgetary year even more than it had originally planned. This seemed to signal that the government still accepted the need for co-ordinating its spending policies with broader economic trends.

The Deficit takes off: from the Brandt and Schmidt years to the unification of Germany

The 1969 general election was one of the turning points in Germany's post-war history (Baring 1984). For the first time a coalition dominated by Socialdemocrats was formed. The party led by Willy Brandt found itself in a fairly complicated situation with regard to future public spending decisions. On the one hand its supporters – not unlike the French President Mitterrand's supporters after his election victory of 1981 (Duhamel 1982) – now expected 'their' government to use its newly won power to enact all the spending programmes for the many groups that had felt neglected by the Conservatives. The majority of these spending programmes were costly social policies. On the other hand the new Minister of Finance, the Socialdemocrat Alex Möller, a fiscal conservative, and Karl Schiller, the Economics Minister, firmly believed in the need for Keynesian demand management. For the early 1970s this meant that the government's primary task was to try to reduce inflationary pressures by limiting public expenditure. So the Socialdemocrats had to make up their minds whether they wanted to please their supporters or whether they preferred budgetary choices which more or less obeyed general economic rules.

The first Brandt Government (1969 to 1972) tried to avoid this dilemma. It made on the one hand concessions to the spending ministries while advocating policies to reduce the money supply. This 'strategy', namely to have it both ways, did not only fail to convince the conflicting interests. Willy Brandt also lost two Economics Ministers (Möller and his successor Schiller). They resigned because they believed that public spending was out of control in a situation where it should have been cut back. Though the economy was in a boom period and needed no additional financial stimulus, the net government borrowing for the fiscal year 1972 was more than double the amount of 1971. Money which had been set aside by a special tax to fight inflation (*Konjunkturzuschlag*) in 1970–1 was not used, as the model of Keynesian demand management would have implied, to repay the deficits incurred at the time of crisis. For fear the voter would misinterpret the intentions of the government the money was given back to the taxpayer in 1972 right before the general election. From a Keynesian economist's point of view this was one of the worst possible decisions the government could have made, because this decision increased economic demand at a time when strong demand had already created high inflation rates.

From hindsight it is impossible to judge whether the new social–liberal coalition of 1974 headed by Chancellor Helmut Schmidt, another Socialdemocrat, would perhaps have had the willpower and the political strength to engage in a more principled course of Keynesian economic steering then the government of his predecessor Brandt. The 1973–4 oil crisis created a completely new framework for economic decision-making worldwide, and the Schmidt Government had to try to cope with this new situation. The quadrupling of oil prices ruined a great number of German firms which were no longer able to compete under the pressure of higher energy prices. A reduced tax income and the cost of greatly increased unemployment reduced the government's budgetary choices and provided a strong incentive for additional deficit-financed spending. In a situation of mass unemployment the government, and especially the biggest party in government, the Socialdemocrats, felt perfectly justified to borrow money for public investments which, it was hoped, would help to create jobs.

The government's strategy to treat the consequences of the oil crisis as if they were a phenomenon similar to the pathologies of the national business cycle proved to be a major logical, political and economic mistake. This mistake was crucial with regard to the growth of public deficits in West Germany in the 1970s (Willms 1988: 105f.). In the aftermath of the oil crisis the Federal Bank (*Bundesbank*) and the German Council of Economic Advisors (*Sachverständigenrat*) had warned against further deficit spending to fight unemployment, because, they argued, the increase of energy prices had shown that certain sectors of Germany's industry lacked competitiveness, but the Schmidt Government still hoped that an increase in public spending, even if it was financed by borrowed money, could kickstart the economy. Between 1975 and 1980 the federal debt grew from 114 billion DM to 232 billion DM. Interest payments increased from 1976: 6.9 billion DM to 1980: 14 billion DM (data in Sturm 1993).

Still, the German economy seemed to be one of the first OECD economies to recover from the oil shock. Between 1976 and 1978 the economy returned to moderate growth rates. For the debt problem this proved to be from hindsight, however, more of a disadvantage than an advantage. During the Bonn G7 economic summit of 1978 the federal government accepted the role of Germany as an 'engine' which should draw the western economies out of the economic quagmire. In practical terms this meant that West Germany was expected to launch a generous spending programme which was supposed to be able to change the general economic climate and to stimulate demand worldwide. The spending programme was financed by new deficits. Unfortunately, this increase of public expenditure had its budgetary effects at an extremely bad moment in time. In 1979–80 Germany was hit – as was the rest of the world – by the second oil crisis, which resulted in further inroads into the competitiveness of German firms, lower tax income and higher spending for the unemployed. Now even the Socialdemocrats had their doubts whether, if one took into account the level of public debt reached in the meantime, governments should go on using borrowed money to buy their way out of an economic crisis which was different in nature from a recession. Though the Schmidt Government began to rearrange its priorities and started a programme of expenditure cuts, the 1980 general election campaign became the first postwar election campaign in Germany which focused on the deficit problem and the public debt.

When the Schmidt Government survived the general election its spending policies were challenged by the opposition in the Constitutional Court – though unsuccessfully, as became clear only much later, in 1989. In 1982 the conflicting views on economic policies of the Liberals and the Socialdemocrats in the governing coalition came to a head. The Liberals had changed their economic philosophy more drastically than the Socialdemocrats had done. While the latter still believed in a global responsibility of the state for a functioning economy the Liberals had begun to regard the maximum freedom of market forces as panacea for all economic ills. For the respective position of the coalition partners on deficits this meant that while Socialdemocrats, though much more hesitantly than in the 1970s, still advocated public spending programmes in order to revive the economy, Liberals wanted to reduce spending in order to fight the deficit. As it turned out these differences in economic philosophies could not be overcome. In 1982 the Liberals decided to form a new coalition government with the Conservatives, the Christian Democrats, who were at that time the party in opposition.

For Germany the 1980s were a period of economic growth. The DM–Dollar exchange rate which favoured the DM facilitated German exports worldwide. This could have been an economic environment conducive to policies of deficit reduction. The growth in tax income and the annual transfers to the federal budget of profits of the Federal Bank (*Bundesbank*) to the tune of 10 billion DM were, however, used only very hesitantly to reduce the accumulated federal debt. The German Government erroneously pretended that it was reducing indebtedness, but it only succeeded in reducing the annual net government borrowing compared to last year's. The new Conservative Government, in other words, did not get out of the habit of borrowing, though for its spending policies it no longer used the Keynesian justification of the state's responsibility for steering the business cycle. Deficits were produced above all by high levels of social spending. The problems of competitiveness of German industry, which had negative effects on the labour market and produced social costs, remained unsolved. Deficits were also unavoidable, because the Conservative Government did not reduce, as it had promised in 1982, the high level of subsidies to German industry (Jákli 1990). In 1988 an increase of financial transfers to the European Union also contributed to the deficit. A three-stage tax reform (1986–90), which was intended to bring German tax levels in line with the tax levels of Germany's major competitors on the world market and which was supposed to provide an incentive for Germany's economic development, created a new shortfall of income for the federal budget.

In the 1980s the annual debt service made up a growing part of the budget. In 1979 5.6 per cent of the annual budget had to be used for paying interest on the federal debt, in 1989 this share of the budget had grown to 11.1 per cent (Schmid 1990: 28). The total of the public debt for all levels of government had been 32.8 per cent of the GDP in 1980 and had grown to over 40 per cent already in 1983. In 1989 the trend to an ever more impressive and potentially economically threatening size of the gross public debt compared to the economy's performance had still not been reversed. The public debt reached 43.6 of the GDP (see Table 4.1). Public opinion in the 1980s was, however, impressed above all by Germany's relative economic growth and the positive climate for German firms at home and abroad. This seemed to have laid the deficit issue to rest. Government rhetoric kept stressing the need for a stricter control of social expenditures. Although because of entitlement laws the growth of the latter was fairly predictable, this had no radical consequences for budgetary policies. There remained a solid level of unemployment to be financed which was immune to the economic boom of the 1980s. The Federal Bank justified the lack of attention paid to the deficit by repeating the old argument that an increase of the debt in absolute terms parallel to the increase of the GDP would do no harm to the economy, because the percentage of the GDP which the debt burden represented, its relative importance, remained stable. The financing of the public debt would, said the Bank, neither crowd out private investments, nor require higher taxation or expenditure cuts.

Table 4.1 Gross public debt (1) and annual net deficits (2) in % of GDP

	(1)	(2)
1980	32.8	2.9
1981	36.5	3.7
1982	39.6	3.3
1983	41.1	2.6
1984	41.7	1.9
1985	42.5	1.2
1986	42.5	1.3
1987	43.8	1.9
1988	44.4	2.2
1989	43.2	0.1
1990	43.6	2.0
1991	41.4 (East Germany: 6.3/West: 43.8)	4.4 (East: 12.7/West: 3.8)
1992	44.0 (East Germany: 14.0/West: 46.5)	3.8 (East: 20.6/West: 2.4)
1993	48.2	3.3
1994	50.4	2.5
1995	58.1	3.5 (a)
1996	60.7	3.8

(a) If the costs caused by the integration of the debt of the *Treuhandanstalt* and East German housing associations into the federal budget were included, the figure would be 9–10% of the GDP.
Sources: Pommerehne and Feld 1994: 57, for 1993ff.: OECD 1996: 28, 33 and for 1996: OECD 1997: 47, 55.

The deficit explodes: German unification and the economic crisis of the 1990s

In 1990 Germany's conservative Minister of Finance, Theo Waigel, claimed in an interview for the weekly magazine *Der Spiegel* (19.11.1990) that without the new costs caused by German unity the net government borrowing of his budget proposals would have been the lowest (measured as percentage of GDP) since 1969. Unity costs were, however, as was well known to the Finance Ministry, unavoidable, though their size and the time period for which financial transfers from West Germany to East Germany were necessary remained controversial. Helmut Kohl, who wanted to secure re-election at the first all-German election in 1990, was joined by influential economists, such as the experts of the research institute of German industry in Cologne (Institut der deutschen Wirtschaft 1990) in predicting that after a brief transition period East Germany would create enough wealth to prosper on self-sustained growth. Therefore transfers were expected to be short-time and limited in size. In practical terms this meant that the government planned to phase out support for East Germany after five years. During these five years the size of transfers was expected to be reduced gradually until it reached the subsidy levels of West German *Länder* (states).

Table 4.2 Net monetary transfers from West to East Germany (in bio. DM)

	1991	1992	1993	1994	1995	1996	1997	1998 (est.)
	106	115	129	125	140	140	136	141
in % of:								
GDP	3.7	3.7	4.1	3.8	4.0	4.0	3.7	3.7
West German GDP	4.0	4.1	4.5	4.2	4.6	4.5	4.2	–
East German GDP	51.5	43.8	41.1	35.3	36.8	35.2	32.2	–

Source: OECD 1998: 69.

For such a brief transition period it seemed justified to finance the take-off period of the East German economy by public deficits. And there was even hope that the benefits of East Germany's economic success would fairly rapidly contribute funds to the task of reducing Germany's public debt. A credit-financed German Unity Fund (*Fonds 'Deutsche Einheit'*) was installed in 1990 which mobilised 115 billion DM for which both the German states and the federal government accepted responsibility. Another justification for the use of credit-financed extra-budgetary funds was the assumption that the assets of the GDR economy sufficed not only to self-finance the programme of privatisation of the GDR economy, but also to cover a good part of the social costs of the transition period from socialism to capitalism (for example the costs of unemployment, pensions or infrastructure investments).

Although numerous models for the calculation of unity costs were developed by economists and economic research institutes, it turned out that most predictions derived from those models were far off the point (Priewe and Hickel 1991: 189ff.). Each financial decision made in the transition period, each strategy employed, had in the end exactly the same overall effect: it increased Germany's total public debt. If one looks for explanations for such serious economic and political misjudgement, it has to be pointed out that unity costs had at least two characteristics, which prevented the application of traditional budgetary planning. One of these characteristics was and still is that unity costs are seen by German decision-makers not only as an economic, but also, and most of the time even more so, as a political and moral problem. The moral problem is contained in the argument that whereas during the forty years before unification West German society enjoyed growing living standards and political freedom the East Germans had to live under a communist dictatorship. The East Germans alone, so the argument goes, had to pay for the presence of Soviet troops in Germany, though the responsibility for the consequences of the Second World War should have been shared by all Germans.

Though West German post-war history was a bit more complicated, and though it may be wrong to classify the personal living conditions of Germans on both sides of the iron curtain simply by the categories 'good' (for the West) and 'bad' (for the

East), it was generally accepted by German politicians that the East Germans had a moral right to living standards comparable to West German ones, and that this aim should be reached as quickly as possible to make up for the time lost. A practical political justification for immediate action was the fact that in 1989 after the Berlin Wall had come down and the border between East and West Germany was opened 344 thousand East Germans immediately left home and resettled in the more prosperous West Germany. This led to the general fear that without an improvement of living conditions in East Germany the depopulation there could not be stopped. In addition to the political pressures exerted by the large number of East–West migrants there was also a legal argument based on Article 72(2) of the German constitution which provided not only an incentive, but an obligation for social and economic 'equalisation' policies. The article stipulates that German governments should provide 'uniform' (since the constitutional reforms of 1994: 'comparable'[3]) living conditions for all Germans.

A second characteristic of unity costs developed after unification over the months and years to come: they proved to be unpredictable. Most observers had fallen victim to economic myths, be it the assumed relative strength of the East German economy which was the leading economy in the communist Eastern bloc, be it the value of assets of East German firms, be it the work ethos of East German workers which was assumed to be kept from developing in the former socialist economy, or be it the benevolent effects of the introduction of a market economy which, it was hoped, would create instant prosperity. What remained of all the wishful thinking was a series of nasty surprises, and an even greater awareness of the size of a problem which seemed extremely difficult to manage. For politicians this meant that there was a constant pressure to mobilise *ad hoc* additional funds for transfer payments to the East without ever being able to see the complete picture and without full knowledge for which purpose investments and social expenditures were really needed and which standards of living, of infrastructure, etc. transfers should be and were able to guarantee.

Though some of the money needed to finance the ongoing annual transfers of more than 150 billion DM from West to East Germany was raised through taxes, even through a special 'solidarity tax' (*Solidaritätszuschlag*), and though public expenditure was cut, the annual net government borrowing remained difficult to control. In addition, there was a rapid growth of deficits hidden in off-budget funds (Burmeister 1997, Gantner 1994). For these off-budget funds legal provisions are possible (and exist) which ignore the deficit limits of Article 115 of the constitution (for details see Burmeister 1997: 227ff.). Special purpose off-budget funds, for example to finance the debt of the railway system (*Bundeseisenbahnvermögen*), a fund which was set up in the course of the planned railway privatisation, or the funds of the successor organisations to the *Treuhand* privatisation agency responsible for the privatisation policies in East Germany, to name just two, contributed and keep contributing to deficit totals. Future obligations not yet reflected in today's deficit figures were accepted by the federal government when it allowed the generous insurance of exports (*Hermes–Kreditversicherungs–AG*), especially to Russia and other former communist countries.

Table 4.3 The development of annual public sector deficits in Germany (in bill. DM)

	1990	1991	1992	1993	1994	1995
Federal government	48.1	53.2	39.3	66.9	50.6	50.5
West German Länder	19.4	16.5	15.9	22.5	24.2	30.0
West German local government	4.2	6.0	9.4	8.9	5.0	12.4
East German Länder	–	12.4	15.1	19.9	19.7	16.6
East German local government	–	1.9	7.5	4.4	5.4	0.8
German Unity Fund	20.0	30.6	22.4	13.5	3.0	2.3
Other funds (1)	2.8	5.9	6.2	1.7	7.5	1.8
Social insurance	+20	+22	2.3	+6.9	+4.3	13.6
Treuhandanstalt	4.3	19.9	29.7	38.1	34.4	–
Public enterprises	9.9	15.6	25.7	20.5	20.2	–

(1) Kreditabwicklungsfonds, ERP-Sondervermögen, Lastenausgleichsfonds, Bundeseisenbahnvermögen, Erblasttilgungsfonds.
Source: OECD 1996: 28.

In the 1990s the debt dynamic produced by the problems of transforming the socialist economy in East Germany into a capitalist one was not kept under control by the performance of the West German economy. On the contrary, the West German economy plunged again into a deep crisis of competitiveness, which provoked government and industry strategies for the country's economic adaption to the new globalised economic world order with high social and economic costs. For public budgets this crisis meant an increase of the annual net government borrowing because of lower tax income and additional social expenditures (especially for unemployment). Other unresolved social and economic problems, such as the size of the public sector, the growing share of the population who are old-age pensioners, or the financial crisis of the health system, also contributed to the budgetary imbalance. So the reasons for a growth of the public debt multiplied. Every economic and social development seemed to point in the same direction. It therefore became politically almost impossible to control expenditures in the short run. The average share of tax income of all levels of government needed to finance debt interests reached 16 per cent in 1995, twice the percentage share needed for this purpose in 1980 (Issing 1996: 196).

In addition, the German Government seemed to lack stamina when it came to the planning and implementation of deficit-reduction policies oriented towards the future. A lowering of aid levels for East Germany might have been popular in West Germany, but it would have made it even more difficult to overcome the psychological and cultural divide between East and West Germans. Radical cuts of subsidies to German industry seemed to run counter to the government's proclaimed aim to help industry in its struggle to defend its position on the world market. Such cuts would have also disadvantaged Germany in the world-wide competition to lure new investors. In addition there are institutional hurdles to radical changes in budgetary policies. For expenditure cuts and changes in the system of taxation in

Table 4.4 Debt totals in the 1990s (in bio. DM)

	1989	**1990**	**1991**	**1992**	**1993**	**1994**	**1995**	**1996**
Total public debt	929	1053	1174	1345	1509	1662	1996	2135
Federal government	491	542	586	611	685	712	757	840
Länder	310	329	352	389	434	471	512	560
Local government	121	126	141	155	173	188	197	205
Special funds	7	57	94	190	217	291	531	531

Source: Deutsche Bundesbank cited in *Die Zeit*, 4.4.97, p. 18.

many cases the consent of a majority of the state governments in the Second Chamber of Parliament (*Bundesrat*) is needed. In the early 1990s it was often impossible to mobilise this majority without the co-operation of the opposition party, the Socialdemocrats. When against all these odds budgetary decisions were made, these decisions were most of the time weak compromises which did not go to the roots of deficit problem.

The budgetary deficits of the mid-1990s were created by a mixture of reduced totals of corporate and income-tax incomes, and the additional expenditures caused by high unemployment. Germany's international companies today pay much less tax than they used to in the past. This is one reason why problems have developed for the accuracy of the government's estimates of tax income. It is no longer the case that the growth of GDP is a good indicator for future tax income. In the 1990s the German Government frequently had to manage with much less than planned tax income. As expenditure planning is mostly based on estimates of tax income such short-falls contribute to new deficits. The stock-taking of the tax experts in 1997, for example, resulted in the prediction of revenue short-falls of 18 billion DM for 1997 and about 30 billion DM in the following years (*Frankfurter Rundschau*, 16.5.1997, p. 1). On the subnational level, the extent of government aid for the long-term unemployed and immigrants (*Sozialhilfe*) and the costs for personnel were the major causes of budgetary imbalances.

Already in 1993 net government borrowing had reached 3.3 per cent of the GDP. This meant that Germany had failed to fulfill one of the criteria – the 3 per cent limit for net government borrowing – which had been laid down in the Maastricht treaty of 1992 for membership in the European Monetary Union. As a consequence the pressures for greater financial discipline of public budgets increased. The German Government together with the French were the driving force behind the idea of a monetary union. From a German perspective monetary union would be unthinkable without the participation of the still strongest European currency, the German Mark. The very strict timetable set for the start of EMU (1999) forced the German Government either to challenge radically the country's welfare consensus or to accept a watering down of the criteria for membership in EMU. The government opted for a muddling-through strategy which even relied on the tricks of 'creative' budgeting to meet the Maastricht criteria. In 1997 the idea of revaluing the gold reserves of the Federal Bank in order to create money for the repayment of debts of the *Erblasttilgungsfonds* (an off-budget fund to repay East German debts), and by doing so enable the government to meet the 3 per cent Maastricht criteria caused a severe conflict between the government and the *Bundesbank*. The compromise found was a revaluation of the federal Dollar reserves in 1998 which has at least some positive effects on the funding of the *Erblasttilgungsfonds*.

In Germany, as in other European countries, the Maastricht criteria provided a (sometimes additional) impetus for deficit control policies. But the social and economic consequences of deficit control policies which led to social unrest also reduced the legitimacy of such policies in the eyes of the citizens. For Germany the fragility of the social consensus which was brought into the open by deficit control policies was a new experience. If the budgetary crisis of the 1990s actually were to give rise to policies which challenge Germany's model of social market capitalism, this would put into question positive assumptions recently made with regard to this model in the general debate on the future of capitalism. It was stated that 'the social market is a self-conscious way for a capitalist economy to blend the gains from competition with those from co-operation' and that 'the social market economy is in the throes of adapting to changed conditions in a unique way' (Hutton 1996: 268). As mentioned, there are already some signs that co-operation and the social elements of the market economy are under severe pressure. Recent government decisions have lowered the tax burden for firms (which increased the deficit), but have at the same time led to several rounds of cuts with regard to social programmes and entitlements (in order both to reduce the deficit and to make up for the tax losses in favour of industry).

Nevertheless the deficit crisis has not abruptly ended Germany's support for the social market economy model. In 1996 a symbolic move was made to find a solution for the current economic problems in the traditional way of co-operation and consensus-building which was given the name 'Alliance for Jobs' (*Bündnis für Arbeit*). The Alliance was made up of representatives of the federal government, the unions and the employer organisations. This latest effort to revive a specific form of German corporatism was supposed to establish a trilateral steering group to bring about the necessary reforms which would create jobs and increase the competitiveness of German industry. But the Alliance failed because the unions were not willing to accept structural changes in the social systems and the employers saw the Alliance only as an instrument to reduce their production costs. Neither a strategic consensus on job creation, nor on competitiveness of German industry nor on debt control policies could be found by the traditional consensus management of German capitalism. This may be interpreted as a further sign for the erosion of social coherence to which the deficit problem contributes.

The institutional framework for decisions on the deficit

The federal government

The federal government prepares the budget decisions and decides on annual net government borrowing. Though in theory Parliament can change the budget the government proposes, in practice a united government which does not suffer from a conflict between its coalition partners is strong enough to guarantee a decision in Parliament which reflects its priorities. To avoid conflict between parties in coalition the extra-constitutional device of a coalition 'treaty' has become the rule (Kropp and Sturm 1998), in which the parties which decide to join forces to form a government lay down the guidelines for this co-operation. This includes also many details of their future policies.

Parliament debates the deficit problem in its budget committee. Though this is traditionally chaired by a representative of the largest party in opposition, the committee's majority is identical with the government majority. Occasionally the government may have to accept defeats and may have to change its spending plans. But the overall decision on the deficit is very unlikely to be reversed here (Sturm 1988). In addition there is a legal restriction for parliamentary initiatives which reduce government income or raise expenditures, either of which may be a method to increase the deficit. Article 113 of the Basic Law, the German constitution, allows such parliamentary initiatives only when they meet with the approval of the government of the day.

German federalism

Compared to other federal political systems German federalism is highly centralised and unitary in character. Instead of a clear separation of the powers of the federal government and the states to spend money and to create income for public budgets, we find a system of 'interlocking federalism'. This means that more than two-thirds of the tax income are raised by joint taxes of the states and the federal government. On the expenditure side more than 50 per cent of laws need the consent of the state governments in the *Bundesrat*, because competences (mostly administrative ones) of the states are affected by federal legislation. The *Bundesrat* is fully involved in the legislative process on the federal level even in the cases where its consent is not needed. With regard to policies only culture (including the media), education and some police powers have remained under control of the states. The vast majority of policy fields are under federal control. However, both the federal government and the state governments decide on their own what the annual net government borrowing should be and determine their own strategies of deficit control. Only local government, which is operating in a framework set by *Land* (state) legislation, has to ask for permission in case it decides to borrow money for financing its expenditures. A regional office of the *Land* acts as supervisory agency for local government borrowing.

The system of interlocking federalism implies a decision-making logic which makes it more likely that deficits are accepted than avoided. For most of the important tax and expenditure decisions a consensus of the state and federal governments is needed. They are most likely to arrive at such a consensus in a situation in which the federal level and each (or most of the) 16 states find advantages for themselves in the decisions to be made. It is obvious that compromises which raise the income of the states and the federal government are easier to achieve than compromises which reduce their income. This means that the decision-making process has an inbuilt structural bias in favour of higher expenditure levels which at least since the 1970s had to be financed by public deficits.

Serious efforts to control or even to reduce the annual deficit create, however, winners and losers. This makes it difficult to come to a consensus, because in the special framework of interlocking federalism simple majorities of one are often too small. Because of constitutional provisions or party political conflicts in the *Bundesrat* even the veto of one *Land* may become magnified in its importance when it withholds the decisive votes needed for a majority in the *Bundesrat*. Such a veto may block all progress for deficit-reduction strategies, be it with regard to changes in the tax code or be it with regard to expenditure cuts. After unification consensus management of German federalism has become even more difficult, because of the new heterogenity between rich and poor and East and West German states (Sturm 1992).

The federal government has tended to call it a success when deficits were reduced on the federal level. This is, however, often achieved by moving expenditures for certain programmes to the *Land* (including the local government) level. From the perspective of the public debt total as it is calculated, for example, when the Maastricht criteria are tested, this is, however, only a cosmetic gain. The shift of responsibility for deficits from one level of government to the other does not reduce Germany's debt total. In 1997 the federal government suggested legislation to define limits of the deficit for each level of government. This initiative was applauded by the rich *Länder* who would be happy to get out of the shared responsibility with the federal government and the poor *Länder*. The latter, as was to be expected, saw insurmountable technical as well as constitutional hurdles for such a move (*Die Zeit*, 9.5.97, p. 24).

The role of the Bundesbank

The *Bundesbank* has no constitutional right to control the deficit. It sees itself in an advisory role with regard to deficit control policies. It accepts, just as another advisory body, the Council of Economic Advisors (*Sachverständigenrat*), the government's right to run a deficit, and it believes the deficit is unproblematic as long as its size corresponds to the dynamics of economic growth. The *Bundesbank* has been contributing to a reduction of the net government borrowing especially since the 1980s by transfers of its annual business profits, not infrequently as big as ten billion DM, to the federal budget.

The *Bundesbank* also plays a prominent role with regard to the interpretation of the deficit for both the government and public opinion. It has regularly identified excessive social spending and subsidisation as sources of the deficit. With regard to strategies which may reduce deficits it has advised the federal government to adhere to economic policies which favour industrial investment (for example by tax reductions) and to cease the redistribution of wealth to the less privileged in society (Tietmeyer 1993).

More important than the *Bundesbank*'s advice are, however, the lessons it draws from deficits for its monetary policies. In the 1980s and well into the 1990s it used to argue that the additional demand of the many levels of German Government for credits led to an expansion of money supply which justified high interest rates. High interest rates in Germany attracted foreign capital which could be used for financing unification costs, for example. For other countries, especially in the European Union, this meant that they also had to operate with high interest rates to stop capital outflows to Germany. Such high interest rates had, however, the negative effect of higher capital costs for their national firms and as a result a reduction of investments and an economic slowdown. In the mid-1990s Germany's interest rates have come down, not the least because of the deep recession the country is in which reduced the demand for capital.

The role of the Federal Constitutional Court

Germany's Federal Constitutional Court only gets involved in political decision-making on budgets if cases are brought before the Court either because of a conflict between branches of government (including the parties in parliament as actors), because courts want final arbitration in principle for specific court cases, or because individuals feel that their civil rights have been violated. In several cases the Court had to judge on the legality of procedures for sharing out financial resources among the states and between the states and the federal government, taking into account the problem of a guaranteed minimum income for the poorer states by a mechanism of financial redistribution between the states. The Court also had to correct tax laws which put an undue burden on the poorer strata of the citizenship and neglected an adequate protection of the well-being of families. All the judgements in the cases mentioned had the effect either of increasing government expenditures or of reducing tax income, and made it more difficult for the government to present a budget which respects the formal limits to borrowing set by the constitution and confirmed by the Constitutional Court. The Court never defined, however, absolute limits for public deficits, though it was asked to do so in 1982 by the joint parliamentary party of the Conservatives (CDU and CSU).

The debt crisis in perspective

For Germans the deficit problem used to conjure up feelings of instability and the fear that irresponsible government expenditure policies could cause inflation. In the collective memory of Germany's post-war generation this fear is connected with the two currency crises of 1923 and 1948 which both led to a currency reform (the introduction of a new currency) and a complete loss of life-time savings. This explains to some extent the cautious use of deficits for financing public expenditures in the first post-war decades. Most of the time the deficit remained below 20 per cent of the annual GNP.

Table 4.5 Public debt in % of GDP

1952	17.1
1955	23.6
1960	17.1
1965	17.6
1970	18.1
1975	24.5
1980	30.7

Source: BMF: Statistische Übersichten zur staatlichen Kreditfinanzierung, in: Diethard B. Simmert and Kurt-Dieter Wagner (eds), *Staatsverschuldung kontrovers,* Köln: Verlag Wissenschaft und Politik 1981, p. 457.

The oil crisis of 1973–4 provoked policies which led to a substantial increase of the deficit, though in international comparison it remained one of the lowest world-wide. In the 1970s the deficit was at first no issue for internal political conflict in Germany. Only in the late 1970s the need for deficit-reduction policies was more widely acknowledged. In the 1980 election campaign the public debt became a topic for party political campaigners. This reflected the fact that after the second world-wide oil crisis in the late 1970s the cut-back strategies became an issue in their own right. The term *Sparpolitik*, meaning policies of austerity, was coined. Differences in the degree and direction of the cut-back management brought down the Socialdemocratic–Liberal coalition of Chancellor Helmut Schmidt in 1982. The economic boom of the 1980s facilitated the control of net government borrowing and helped to avoid a radical application of cut-back strategies. Since 1991, shortly after the first all-German election, a new period of *Sparpolitik* began, introducing the longest, but also the most radical period of deficit control policies in German post-war history.

Expenditures for German unification and recently the Maastricht criteria have given a new meaning to the deficit 'problem'. The financing of German unification has created a permanent drain on public finances for the foreseeable future. The OECD (1997: 57) estimates that about half the increase in public debt since 1989 has been caused by German unification. This has eroded the hope for a swift return to more balanced budgets. The Maastricht criteria have greatly increased the pressure on budgeting and have reinstated financial discipline as a public policy virtue. As never before the social consequences of deficit-reduction policies have brought home the fact to every single German that deficits are no longer about abstract numbers, but phenomena of a highly topical and politically relevant nature.

In 1997 the planned budget total of the federal budget was 439.9 billion DM; 127.8 billion were to be spent by the Ministry for Employment and Social Affairs, 86.0 billion were needed to service the federal debt and only 46.3 billion were to be spent on defence. In his 1997 report to the EU Finance Ministers the German Finance Minister, Theo Waigel, for the first time cited the costs of German unity to explain Germany's problems with the Maastricht criteria. In this Minister Waigel was supported by the *Bundesbank*. The *Bundesbank* repeated, however, its general warning that Germany may be already or very soon a victim of the 'debt trap', i.e. the country is in danger of using up all the borrowed money (and more) just to pay for interest on the public debt.

Deficit control policies

Germany never developed a coherent set of deficit control policies. The German constitution is in principle fairly clear on the limits of deficits. As mentioned above, its Article 115 stipulates that the deficit totals in a budget should not exceed the total of investment expenditures. Exceptions are, however, possible if and when the economy is in a status of 'imbalance' (*Störung des gesamtwirtschaftlichen Gleichgewichts*). Article 115 in its present form is a brainchild of Keynesian economic thought which was in fashion in Germany from the mid-1960s to the mid-1970s. During this period the necessary two-third majorities in both Houses of Parliament could be found to change the constitution accordingly. Today the economic consensus in Germany has changed, but for reasons of party political conflict no new two-third majorities have been brought together to rewrite the constitution. What has happened is that on the one hand the constitutional provisions allowing governments to steer macro-economic developments were ignored, but on the other hand the governments remain grateful for the flexibility the existing provisions provide with regard to the size of the annual deficit.

In 1989 the Constitutional Court in its judgement on the constitutionality of the 1981 federal budget added a few details to the broad definition of limits for public deficits found in the constitution (BVerfG 1989). The Court criticised the loose way in which the term investment was defined, namely either as every capital flow which in a macro-economic perspective improves an economy's assets, or simply as equivalent to certain chapters of the budget papers. The Court made it the duty of Parliament to develop a more precise definition of investments. The result of such a clearer definition should be, so the Court argued, to avoid increases in the public debt whenever possible. So far, neither Parliament nor the government have reacted to the Court's demand.

On the fact that in cases of budgetary imbalance the size of investments is no longer the yardstick for the annual deficit, the Court's comments were cautious. It stressed that the government's analysis of current economic problems and its conclusions have to be accepted. This analysis should, however, be made explicit in the budget papers. And it should be based on all political and economic information available (including the work of the leading German economic research institutes and economists and the *Bundesbank*) in order to eliminate every trait of arbitrariness.

So far German politicians have payed only formal lip service to the Court's rulings. Paragraph 18 of the law on budgeting (*Bundeshaushaltsordnung*) was changed in 1990. It now incorporates the Court's demand for explications when governments claim that an economic crisis situation made it impossible to avoid deficits in a given year. In practice no change in the procedure of budgeting or in the way deficits are legitimised can be observed, however. For some time politicians of all parties seemed to have had severe doubts whether the Court should ever be given a chance again to rule on limits for the annual deficit. The Conservatives who were the initiators of the Court's first ruling after they had become a party in government were extremely worried that the Court's ruling might declare some of their budgets unconstitutional, too. All politicians abhor the idea that when they spend DMs the Court constantly looks over their shoulder. Still in 1997 the Socialdemocrats, the leading party in opposition, challenged the 1996 federal budget at the Federal Constitutional Court. The Socialdemocrats argued that the government now routinely ignores the deficit limit (size of investments) and must therefore be stopped by the Court if Parliament cannot do it.

Although in some states (Bavaria, Baden-Württemberg) the idea of a balanced budget found support in the 1980s, the necessary adjustments to budgetary policy-making were at best made tentatively. The federal government (when it saw the growing public debt as a problem at all) sought only to reduce the current net government borrowing compared to last year's. Some cut-back policies were started in the mid-1970s as a reaction to the increased expenditures to finance structural unemployment caused by the lack of competitiveness in German industry as a result of the oil shock, but it would be an exaggeration to argue that these cuts had in a major way affected the development of the public debt. Deficit-reduction policies remained incremental even in the rare years when they were efficient. Only the Maastricht criteria defined clear aims for deficit control, but when confronted with those aims the government remained unable to develop strategies for coping systematically with the public debt problem. An indicator for the dilemma the government is in has been the frequent use of the instrument of budget implementation controls (*Haushaltssperre*) by the Minister of Finance. This instrument makes every single item of departmental spending from a certain size upwards dependent on the permission of the Minister of Finance. In this way deficit problems are postponed, but remain unsolved. There is, however, a new challenge ahead. The federal government and the *Länder* have to find a procedure for co-ordinating their expenditure policies after Germany has entered the European Monetary Union. Only a national 'stability pact' will guarantee that public spending in Germany (which includes, of course, public spending on all levels of government) will in the future respect the limits set by the Maastricht criteria.

Deficits – the German experience

Post-war Germany only had a negligible deficit. Today a former President of the Federal Bank, Helmut Schlesinger, sees the country caught in a debt trap. What has happened during the past fifty years?

The history of the deficit problem in Germany documents a slow but permanent increase of the public debt since the mid-1960s. Public debt was at first the side-effect of government overspending, but was with the advent of Keynesianism in Germany for some time even seen as a kind of virtue. A grand coalition of parties, voters and economists who all relied on Germany's economic strength for a long time closed their eyes on the long-term effects of deficits. Unfortunately no legal or constitutional provision stopped the spenders. When Germany realised how much debt it had already piled up the economic situation had changed for the worse. A quick return to lower levels of public debt seemed to be impossible. Cut-backs in social expenditures and the economic boom of the 1980s helped to stabilise the situation. Germany could draw some comfort from the fact that it had in comparison to other EU countries a fairly low public debt measured as share of its GDP.

The situation changed, however, dramatically in the 1990s. The combination of economic crisis, increasing social expenditures (because of this crisis, but also for other reasons, such as migration to Germany or the ageing of the population), tax avoidance of Germany's still very successful multi-national companies in order to improve shareholder values and the costs of German unification resulted in a rapid deterioration of budgetary stability. As clearly as never before the budgetary dilemmas of German decision-makers were brought into the spotlight by the parallel process of European monetary integration. The Maastricht criteria challenge current tax and expenditure policies more than the weak constitutional limits to the deficit. The latter stipulate that annual net public borrowing should not be higher than the spending on investments, except in a situation of economic crisis. Even the Constitutional Court has not suceeded in finding hard and fast criteria, however, to transform the words of the constitution into a weapon with which politicians can successfully be kept away from excessive borrowing. In the 1990s the federal government frequently not only borrowed more than it officially invested (Sturm 1998). What is even more worrying is that the amount of money borrowed did not even suffice to pay the interest on the federal debt. With the Maastricht criteria in place which Germany is only just able to meet, the room for new deficits has become extremely limited. After the 1998 general election hard choices seem to be difficult to avoid both with regard to public expenditures and with regard to deficit control on the federal and the *Land* level of government.

There is no easy way out of this situation. Public opinion and interest groups in Germany strongly oppose expenditure cuts. Tax reform has become the victim of institutional inertia. And there is no sign of a resurrection of the old tax base or of an economic recovery in East Germany. For Germany the debt problem has become synonymous with a challenge to its traditional and cherished social market economy. Deficits are today a symptom of its malfunctioning. A serious attempt to cope with the deficit problem in Germany has as its pre-condition a change in the political culture of the country and a modernisation of its economy – a task which is not made easier by the continuing division of the country between West and East.

Notes

1. For the following see in greater detail Sturm 1993.
2. Most of the surplus was set aside for the planned build-up of armed forces (the *Bundeswehr*).
3. The German equivalents are *'einheitlich'* and *'gleichwertig'*.

Reference

Abelshauser, Werner (1983) *Wirtschaftsgeschichte der Bundesrepublik Deutschland, 1945–1980*, Frankfurt am Main: Suhrkamp.

Baring, Arnulf (1984) *Machtwechsel. Die Ära Brandt–Scheel*, München: dtv.

Burmeister, Kerstin (1997) *Außerbudgetäre Aktivitäten des Bundes. Eine Analyse der Nebenhaushalte des Bundes unter besonderer Berücksichtigung der finanzhistorischen Entwicklung*, Frankfurt: Lang.

BVerfG (Bundesverfassungsgericht) (1989) *Entscheidungen*, vol. 79, Tübingen: Mohr.

Duhamel, Alain (1982) *La République de M. Mitterrand*, Paris: Bernard Grasset.

Gantner, Manfried (Hrsg.) (1994) *Budgetausgliederungen – Fluch(t) oder Segen?*, Wien: Manz.

Hutton, Will (1996) *The State We're In*, London: Vintage.

Institut der deutschen Wirtschaft (1990) *Wirtschaftliche und soziale Perspektiven der deutschen Einheit*, Cologne: Institut der deutschen Wirtschaft.

Issing, Otmar (1996) 'Staatsverschuldung als Generationenproblem', in: Immenga, Ulrich, Möschel, Wernhard and Reuter, Dieter (eds), *Festschrift für Ernst-Joachim Mestmäcker*, Baden-Baden: Nomos, pp. 191–209.

Jákli, Zoltán (1990) *Vom Marshallplan zum Kohlepfennig. Grundrisse der Subventionspolitik in der Bundesrepublik Deutschland 1948–1982*, Opladen: Westdeutscher Verlag.

Kropp, Sabine and Sturm, Roland (1998) *Koalitionsvereinbarungen in den Bundesländern. Analyse und Dokumentation*, Opladen: Leske und Budrich.

Lutz, Burkhart (1984) *Der kurze Traum immerwährender Prosperität. Eine Neuinterpretation der industriell-kapitalistischen Entwicklung im Europa des 20. Jahrhunderts*, Frankfurt am Main: Campus.

Möller, Alex and Schwebler, Robert (n.d.) *Schuld durch Schulden? Nutzen und Grenzen der Staatsverschuldung*, München and Zürich: Droemer Knaur.

OECD (1996) *Wirtschaftsberichte (Deutschland)*, Paris: OECD.

OECD (1997) *Wirtschaftsberichte (Deutschland)*, Paris: OECD.

OECD (1998) *Wirtschaftsberichte (Deutschland)*, Paris: OECD.

Pommerehne, Werner W. and Feld, Lars P. (1994) 'Fiscal evolution of the Federal Republic of Germany, 1980–92: recent developments and room for consolidation', in: *European Economy* 3, pp. 47–95.

Priewe, Jan and Hickel, Rudolf (1991) *Der Preis der Einheit. Bilanz und Perspektiven der deutschen Vereinigung*, Frankfurt am Main: Fischer.

Schlesinger, Helmut, Weber, Manfred and Ziebarth, Gerhard (1991) *Gesamtstaatliche Finanzpolitik in der Bewährung*, Tübingen: Walter Eucken Institut.

Schmid, Klaus-Peter (1990) 'Der gefesselte Staat. Weil der Finanzminister immer mehr Zinsen zahlen muß, fehlt Geld für andere Aufgaben', in: *Die Zeit*, 28 Sept., p. 28.

Sturm, Roland (1988) *Der Haushaltsausschuß des Deutschen Bundestages*, Opladen: Leske und Budrich.

Sturm, Roland (1989) *Haushaltspolitik in westlichen Demokratien. Ein Vergleich des haushaltspolitischen Entscheidungsprozesses in der Bundesrepublik Deutschland, Frankreich, Großbritannien, Kanada und den USA*, Baden-Baden: Nomos.

Sturm, Roland (1992) 'The changing territorial balance', in: Smith, Gordon, Paterson, William E., Merkl, Peter H. and Padgett, Stephen (eds), *Developments in German Politics*, Basingstoke and London: Macmillan, pp. 119–34.

Sturm, Roland (1993) *Staatsverschuldung. Ursachen, Wirkungen und Grenzen staatlicher Verschuldungspolitik*, Opladen: Leske und Budrich.

Sturm, Roland (1994) 'Budgeting as informed guess work: has the German budgetary process lost direction?, in: *Public Budgeting and Financial Management* 6(1), pp. 130–53.

Sturm, Roland (1998) 'Die Wende im Stolperschritt – eine finanzpolitische Bilanz', in: Wewer, Göttrik (ed.), *Bilanz der Ära Kohl*, Opladen: Leske und Budrich, pp. 183–200.

Tietmeyer, Hans (1993) 'In welchem Umfang darf sich ein Staat verschulden?', in: *Aus Politik und Zeitgeschichte* 18, pp. 13–18.

Willms, Manfred (1988) 'Public debt and public debt policy in Germany', in: Cavanna, Henri (ed.), *Public Sector Deficits in OECD Countries. Causes, Consequences and Remedies*, Basingstoke and London: Macmillan, pp. 102–19.

Chapter 5

United States of America

The history of the deficit problem

Public deficits are a permanent feature of American economic history. Their origins and contexts are, however, diverse and keep changing. The deficit problem is strongly related to the institutional framework which controls budgeting – and this is the case in the United States more so than in any other of the countries whose history of the deficit we have analysed. In addition to institutional arrangements ideological conflict over deficits matters, too, when it comes to decisions on budgetary policies. Sometimes both aspects overlap in their effects on budgetary decisions, sometimes they neutralise each other. A third factor which explains deficits in the United States, external pressures, should also be mentioned here. The first part of this chapter will try to explain the interplay of these three different causes for deficits in American history.

The colonial period and the founding of a nation

Contrary to what proponents of balanced budgets claim, there has never been a consensus in favour of balanced budgets in American history. Colonial governments in the early period of European settlement in America tended to use instruments of deficit spending in pursuit of political and economic goals. There were three categories of aims to be distinguished: financing military actions (Burdekin and Langdana 1992: xxii), counterbalancing costs resulting from recessions or economic problems in general, and financing the outflow of gold to England, which in those days was caused by the colonial terms of trade (Savage 1990: 59). The instruments for financing the deficit used at the time were different from those used today. Colonial governments issued paper money, the so-called bills of credit, not only to create a means of payment, but also to borrow money from the public. The inflationary consequences of expanding the volume of paper money was known quite well and investors have always criticised this policy (Savage 1990: 61).

Issuing bills of credit was also the main instrument for financing the Revolutionary War against England. Then colonial, now state governments even waived any legal restrictions to the limit of credit, since the value of the state 'currencies' was remarkably stable (Savage 1990: 66). Moreover, constitutional restrictions for bills of credit on the state level did not come into effect until 1840.

However, the record of the 'Continental', the name of a bill of credit issued after 1775, was far from perfect. Its value decreased enormously till 1780, when the Continental Congress decided to reduce its value. This disaster had occurred because, first, the expansion of its volume was excessive and second, the Continental was never considered a 'currency', thus was never used as a means of payment, but was simply seen as an investment opportunity for wealthy citizens and foreign investors. Its failure put pressure on the states to take responsibility and to finance the war. The states were asked to increase their contributions to the federal budget, and to finance this increase by higher taxes. As in our days, state governments were reluctant to put an additional burden on their constituencies, thus denying the federal government help when it was most needed. Savage claims that it was this problem of financing the war against England which contributed heavily to pressures on the states during the negotiations on a new constitution that ultimately resulted in enhanced sources of income for the federal government (Savage 1990: 67). Hamilton and Madison, in particular, realised that the federal government needed such sources of income and argued that the issuance of paper money alone was not a sufficient instrument to sustain the federal government (Rossiter 1961).

Even in this pre-constitutional period it seemed clear that other points of contention were also at stake with regard to public expenditure. The central question seemed to be: which government is ultimately sovereign? Granting the power to issue paper money and to borrow from the financial markets to the federal government would decide this question in its favour. Leaving these powers with the states would imply that the federal level remained some kind of 'confederation', a supranational entity that would break up as soon as the reason for its creation disappeared. The founding fathers decided in Article 1, Section 10 of the American Constitution that the states must lose their power to issue bills of credit, which meant they also lost their instrument for borrowing from the market. We can hardly overestimate the significance of this decision for the evolution of American federalism and American governance in general.

Thus the history of the United States of America begins with public deficits. The costs of war generated a national debt of 77 million dollars. To cope with this problem during the first few years of the newly-founded republic cautious budgetary policies were needed. The first 'gridlock' in federal budgetary policy occurred as a result of ill-divided competences between the states and the Continental Congress. This gridlock caused a transfer of financial powers from the states to the federal government.

The heritage of a national debt of 77 million dollars, accumulated during the Revolutionary War, was neither reduced nor increased during the first decade of American history (Anderson 1987: 10). In the nineteenth century budget surpluses were the rule, and deficits only occurred in times of economic or military crises.

This successful attempt to balance the budget can be attributed to Secretary of the Treasury Alexander Hamilton, the first officeholder. According to one author, Hamilton served as the actual 'head' of the Washington administration (Croly 1909: 38). He aimed at an 'executive budget', while President George Washington apparently developed little interest in such attempts of his Secretary of the Treasury. Buck summarised this extremely important period of American constitutional formation as follows (Buck 1929: 17):

> jealousy between the legislative and executive branch of the government became so intensified that Congress sought executive decentralization in budgetary matters. In this situation the President did not insist upon the exercise of his evident constitutional right to prepare a budget as an administrative proposal, hence the budgetary powers passed to congressional committees. Thus budget making became an exclusively legislative function in the national government and as such it continued for more than a century.

Of course, Congress was granted the 'power of the purse' by Article 1, Section 9, of the US Constitution, which reads 'No Money shall be drawn from the Treasury, but in Consequence of Appropriations made by Law'. However, the founding fathers hardly intended to create an exclusive power for Congress. One can only speculate what would have happened if Madisonian Budgeting, as White and Wildavsky called it (White and Wildavsky 1989: 1), had been overturned by Hamiltonian Budgeting.

One of the most striking institutional features of this period was the high degree of centralisation of budget decisions, which were made in only one committee in both the House and the Senate. The House Ways and Means Committee was there from the start, the Senate Finance Committee was created in 1816. Both served as the central committees for decisions on revenues as well as on spending (Shuman 1992: 76). They continued in this extraordinary function till 1865 and 1867 respectively (Cogan 1994: 29). Cogan argues that there was a correlation of empirical significance between centralisation of budgetary decision-making in Congress and balanced budgets. There was indeed a significant increase of the national debt around the time when both committees lost their powerful positions. Nevertheless, since this was a period of radical change in the United States (after all, we are talking about the years of the Civil War and its aftermath), Cogan's hypothesis needs further examination.

Hamilton, the federalist, and his political enemy Jefferson, the anti-federalist and defender of balanced budgets, agreed on a policy of balanced budgets. Their differences lay beneath the surface. In terms of modern political discourse, the controversy of Jefferson and Hamilton parallels today's 'big government' versus 'small government' disputes. Hamilton always favoured free access to financial markets for the federal government during times of war and peace (Cooke 1964: 2). He considered fiscal independence a prerequisite for sovereignty, even if he himself as Secretary of the Treasury favoured a cautious use of these new powers in order to strengthen the credit record of the federal government (Kimmel 1959: 9). Balanced budgets were not considered a goal in their own right, but as a means to establish a strong federal government (Savage 1990). Jefferson feared 'that a central government burdened by deficits and debts would undermine its republican and constitutional foundations while it promoted widespread social and economic inequality' (Savage 1990: 95). Thus, he favoured a Balanced Budget Amendment. (He was the first supporter of this principle in a long line of proponents of constitutional restrictions on federal budgeting.) Jefferson intended to weaken the central government, and to secure for the states as many powers as possible. The ideal he had in mind was an agrarian state, full of opportunities for all free citizens (Kimmel 1959: 16). As a consequence he agreed to the purchase of Louisiana, in order to promote the expansion of agrarian America (Savage 1992: 5), even if this meant that borrowing from financial markets was necessary to finance such a deal.

Jefferson used not only political arguments, but also moral ones. Public debt, he argued, represents an illegitimate burden on future generations. If there is a need to go into deficit, we ought to pay it back ourselves (Malone 1951: 179). Astonishingly enough, Jefferson was much less concerned about state deficit spending (Savage 1992: 5). His bias towards strong states and a weak central government made him ignore this inconsistency in his line of argument. Budgeting in the United States has never been a question of good or bad policy, but has always been based on specific conceptions of the state. The controversy between Hamilton and Jefferson in the early years of the history of the United States illustrates the conflicting views which came to dominate political struggles in budgetary matters. It can be interpreted as the first of many conflicts beween proponents of balanced budgets and of deficit spending.

Consolidation of the state: from Madison to Buchanan

In the years between the Jefferson presidency and the Civil War, the United States enjoyed a period of fiscal stability. From 1816 to 1862, there were only 17 deficits, 2 of which were under one million dollars, thus negligible. Most deficits occurred before wars (Savage 1990: 288), and in virtually all cases they were attributable to war, economic recession and financial panics. When there were budget surpluses, they were used to pay back the national debt. In 1834–5 the total gross debt was only $38,000.

Decision-making on spending and taxation was still centralised in the standing Senate Finance and the House Ways and Means Committees respectively. From time to time non-standing committees, the so-called expenditure committees, were established in order to decide on crucial budgets like the ones of the army, navy, treasury or of the US mail service. In 1837 the House of Representatives (and in 1850 the Senate) passed new internal rules which created the still existing distinction between the authorisation and appropriation of expenditures (Shuman 1992: 76). Ever since, any appropriation of resources (by an appropriations committee) needs an earlier authorisation (by a legislative committee) that specifies the intended policy in the given issue area. Though these institutional changes greatly influenced federal budgeting, they had no dramatic effect on public deficits.

In the first half of the nineteenth century clearly distinguishable political positions on public debts emerged. Three of them seem to be interesting and important enough for our general topic to be worth mentioning here. The first influential view of interest is the one held by President Andrew Jackson, a radical enemy not only of public deficits, but also of borrowing in general. As a young man, Jackson was almost ruined by one of his debtors. Later, he developed a strong aversion against banks and other financial institutions, including their owners (Savage 1990: 103). His position was different from Jefferson's. Jefferson was concerned about the federal government which he feared might get too powerful; in other words, he was worried about a question of power and democracy. Jackson, on the other hand, was more concerned about the loyalty of the people to the state when confronted with economic hardship resulting from budget deficits (Kimmel 1959: 19). Moreover, deficits were considered a burden especially for the working classes, since interest payments on the national debt were seen as a redistribution of wealth in favour of the well-to-do.

The second influential view on public debts was developed by Jackson as well, and was later brought forward in a more pronounced fashion by James K. Polk and James Buchanan: American Government needs the trust and respect of other countries. Thus, sound budgetary policies are required. We find this idea in Polk's strength-among-nations argument as well as in Buchanan's preservation-of-the-public-credit argument (Kimmel 1959: 23ff.). However, there is more to this second position than pure diplomatic pragmatism. President Martin van Buren's concern about budget surpluses during his time in office was caused by signs of over-taxation and government inefficiency. This shows that the older idea of distrust in government was still dominant. When after the 1839 recession financial difficulties became apparent, van Buren refused both to raise taxes and to increase public debt. Kimmel has summarised van Buren's rationale (Kimmel 1959: 25):

> The official position was that no circumstances could justify deficits in time of peace. Under no conditions should the citizen look to the government for aid to relieve embarrassments arising from losses by 'revulsions' in commerce and credit.

This conception of the role of the state has later been called the 'nightwatchman state', and it summarises the essence of conservativism and laissez-faire in its most extreme form.

In the early nineteenth century, mainstream arguments in economics had just begun to change. The unconditional aversion against unbalanced budgets as expressed by many economists from Adam Smith to Karl Marx (Fink and High 1987) had now shifted somewhat to less dogmatic assessments (Kimmel 1959: 38ff.). President John Adams was one of the first presidents to stress the need for financial support of the process of growing together, a strategy which included all fiscal options, i.e. also public deficits. The legitimacy of government support for internal improvements (of infrastructure) had long been recognised before (Kimmel 1959: 29), but Adams now noted explicitly that there was a trade-off between the political objectives of balanced budgets and internal improvements. It was the first attempt to introduce economically 'rational' arguments into the debate on the deficit dealing with it as a question of optimal fiscal management that needs to be assessed with regard to the policies pursued. However, moral arguments and symbolic politics still remained dominant in this debate.

Discovering the state: from Lincoln to Hoover

The Civil War and the events preceeding it resulted in the largest relative increase in public debt so far in American history (Anderson 1987: 12ff.). The total gross debt rose from about 90 million dollars in 1861 to 2.6 billion dollars in 1864 (Savage 1990: 288). Budget surpluses during the following years till the 1890s then contributed to a nominal and real (if measured as debt-to-GNP ratio) debt reduction. In the upcoming decades before the First World War, three recessions in 1904, 1908 and 1912 again caused deficits (Anderson 1987: 12). The First World War brought with it a rise in the national debt from 1.2 billion dollars in 1916 to as much as 25.5 billion dollars in 1919 (Savage 1990: 289). The inter-war years and their surpluses helped reduce this immense figure to 16.2 billion. Considering the debt-to-GNP ratio, the national debt was reduced by 40 per cent (Anderson 1987: 13).

These simple figures seem to indicate that general budgetary norms – deficits are acceptable only in times of war, economic crises or other kinds of catastrophies – had not changed. Deficits correlate with times of recession or times of war, surpluses occurred in times of peace and prosperity. Such an assumption would, however, be misleading. In fact, this was a period of American fiscal history which brought about some of the most fundamental changes in fiscal and tax policies. Abraham Lincoln's presidency marks the departure from Jeffersonian federal laissez-faire policy and Jefferson's small-government doctrine to the beginning of the move to Franklin Roosevelt's New Deal, which incorporated basic ideas of Keynesian economic policy (Kimmel 1959: 61). Partly, this change was due to Lincoln's personal belief that public debts do not matter, since they constitute a liability to one's own people (Savage 1990: 128), partly there were unavoidable pressures to go into debt to finance the Civil War and the reconstruction of the country in its aftermath. Lincoln's presidency revolutionised American fiscal policy (Kimmel 1959: 64).

In 1863 a national banking system was established and thus the opportunity for the effective marketing of government bonds was created. At about the same time tax laws made US bank-notes the only legal means of payment (Myers 1970: 162ff.). Even more important a national income tax was introduced and tariffs and duties were increased (Anderson 1987: 16ff.). Now the state had the resources it needed to intensify and extend its activities. Savage argues that the big budgetary surpluses in the post-Civil War years were due to increased revenues from tariffs and duties (Savage 1990: 122). The old 'virtue' of small government seemed forgotten and now it was taken for granted that the budget had to be balanced by increased expenditures instead of a reduction in revenues.

There are two main arguments which explain the reluctance of Lincoln and his successors to reduce tariffs. First, tariffs can be considered as an instrument of protectionism against foreign products, a fact which at the time made them attractive to corporate America (Savage 1990: 123 and 142). Secondly, and this explanation has been favoured by many economists, the years between the Civil War and the First World War were a period of transition; a new consensus emerged with regard to the political and economic role of the state in people's lives. The federal government saw both the necessity to rebuild and improve infrastructure, especially in the South (Keller 1977), and a strong need to regulate parts of the national economy (Kimmel 1959: 78). This is the time when first steps in anti-trust legislation were taken (McCraw 1984). In short, the need for greater government activity was accepted, and this in turn legitimised an increase of revenues for the federal government.

Lincoln's successors in office were more concerned about the implied growth of the federal government than he was (Kimmel 1959: 68). However, the Growth-of-Nation argument also provided critics of federal activism with an argument which allowed them to see the repayment of the national debt as an issue of only secondary importance. The early twentieth century witnessed, if we use a fairly crude yardstick, three different 'types' of presidents. Theodore Roosevelt and Robert Taft were inclined to see state intervention positively, Calvin Coolidge, Warren G. Harding and Herbert C. Hoover were more conservative in this respect, and Woodrow Wilson, perhaps the most intriguing figure of that time, stood alone. Wilson's approach to 'new politics' as a compromise of socialism and laissez-faire (Kimmel 1959: 87) made an important contribution to a revised understanding of the role of the federal government. Moreover, Wilson developed the idea of a neutral, professional administration, separated from politics, that is free to do 'good' work for the people (Koven 1988: 168). Strongly influenced by economics and scientific management, Wilson and others were looking for new efficient and rational strategies to solve practical problems. This was one of the first attempts to 'depoliticise' politics. We will see that attempts to control the budget today, such as the balanced budget amendment to the Constitution, owe much to the idea of getting politics out of budgetary policies. Furthermore, as shall be argued in part three of this chapter, Wilson's management techniques reappeared later in the century.

The political process of budgeting had been decentralised throughout the nineteenth century. First, appropriations committees were established in the mid-1860s, followed by a widening of Congressional budgetary competences through the setting up of other committees (Cogan 1994: 29ff.). Cogan argues that there was a correlation between such reforms of the internal organisation of Congress and the growth of public activity since the mid-1850s (Cogan 1994: 30ff.). For example, where Congress established legislative committees to decide upon spending in certain issue areas, spending increased enormously. When budgetary competences were reunified after the First World War we observe a relative decrease of federal spending, and budget surpluses occurred once again (Cogan 1994: 35ff.). The Budget and Accounting Act was passed by Congress in 1921. This Act changed the process of budgeting fundamentally. It gave it the shape it basically still has today. The Act provided for a major role of the executive branch in budgetary matters. From now on it became difficult to distinguish between effects on budgetary results due to internal reforms of Congress and effects due to the new 'balance of power' among the branches of government.

The fiscal (r)evolution: the New Deal and its aftermath

Dramatic shifts in budgeting, budgetary politics and budgetary policies took place in the period from 1932 to the present. The US national debt virtually exploded nominally, yet in terms of real growth its increase was less spectacular. The Second World War caused a debt increase unmatched by any growth of the deficit until the 1980s, if deficits are measured in relation to the GNP (Ippolito 1990: 5). The national debt as percentage of the GNP grew from 17.8 per cent in 1930 to 134.2 per cent by the end of the Second World War. Between 1950 and 1980, this figure fell to its post-war minimum of 35.5 per cent, but then started to rise again (Anderson 1987: 13ff.). Ever since, the United States has been experiencing a rapid growth of deficits in nominal and in real terms, despite the limited success of counter-measures intended to stop its growth, e.g. the Gramm–Rudman–Hollings Act (1985) (Saturno 1994: 4). The gross national debt total has not been reduced since 1949. For many students of budgeting, the obvious inability of the federal government to do so is the most outstanding characteristic of the US budgetary process (Rabushka 1988: 186).

In terms of institutional change budgetary politics since the 1930s may be characterised as suffering from the increased decentralisation of decision-making in Congress. In 1932 the House and Senate appropriations committees were in control

Table 5.1 Federal deficits and total gross debt 1930–97

Fiscal year	Deficit (billion dollars)	Total gross debt (bn)
1930	0.7 (surplus)	16.19
1931	0.5	16.80
1932	2.7	19.49
1933	2.6	22.54
1934	3.6	27.05
1935	2.8	28.70
1936	4.4	33.78
1937	2.8	36.42
1938	1.2	37.16
1939	3.9	40.44
1940	3.9	42.97
1941	6.2	48.96
1942	20.8	72.4
1943	54.9	136.7
1944	47.0	201.0
1945	47.5	258.7
1946	15.9	269.4
1947	3.9 (surplus)	258.3
1948	12.0 (surplus)	252.3
1949	0.6 (surplus)	257.4
1950	3.1	257.4
1951	6.1 (surplus)	255.2
1952	1.5	259.1

Table 5.1 (*cont'd*)

Fiscal year	Deficit (billion dollars)	Total gross debt (bn)
1953	6.5	266.1
1954	1.2	270.8
1955	3.0	274.4
1956	4.1 (surplus)	272.8
1957	3.2 (surplus)	272.4
1958	2.9	279.7
1959	12.9	287.8
1960	0.3 (surplus)	290.9
1961	3.4	292.9
1962	7.1	303.3
1963	4.7	310.8
1964	5.9	316.8
1965	1.6	323.2
1966	3.8	329.5
1967	8.7	341.3
1968	25.2	369.8
1969	3.2 (surplus)	367.1
1970	2.8	382.6
1971	23.0	409.5
1972	23.4	437.3
1973	14.8	468.4
1974	4.7	486.2
1975	45.1	544.1
1976	66.4	631.9
1977	57.9	709.1
1978	48.8	780.4
1979	27.7	833.8
1980	59.6	914.3
1981	57.9	1003.9
1982	110.6	1147.0
1983	195.4	1381.9
1984	175.4	1576.7
1985	212.2	1788.9
1986	221.2	2010.1
1987	149.8	2159.9
1988	155.2	2315.1
1989	152.5	2467.6
1990	221.4	2689.0
1991	269.5	2958.5
1992	290.4	3248.9
1993	254.7	3503.6
1994	203.2	3706.8
1995	163.9	3870.7
1996	107.3	–
1997	126.0 (est.)	–

Sources: Savage 1990, appendix (until 1984), OECD 1996 and 1996a (deficits 1985–1995), *The Economist*, 1.2.1997: 56 (deficit 1996), *Financial Times*, 7.2.1997: 5 (deficit 1997 est.) and author's calculation (debt 1985–95).

of about 89 per cent of all government spending. This figure fell to 63 per cent in 1992 (Cogan 1994: 23). How did this change come about? Three developments are crucial here.

First, as early as 1932, the Reconstruction Finance Corporation (RFC) was granted the so-called 'borrowing authority', which means that this institution was given the right to go directly to the US Treasury and request funding. Borrowing authority expanded rapidly and was extended to diverse issue areas and committees (Cogan 1994: 14).

Second, with the reform policies of the New Deal, entitlement spending increased dramatically. The federal government opened up pension funds, formerly reserved for federal public servants, to the general public (social security). Funding for Aid to Families with Dependent Children, Medicare and Medicaid and Guaranteed Student Loans has been provided since the 1930s. President Lyndon B. Johnson's Great Society programme of the 1960s initiated additional efforts of the federal government to improve public welfare, education and other fields of social policy. These programmes also indicate a strategic shift from financing policy initiatives through general funds to the use of trust funds for this purpose, thus 'crowding out' the former in favour of the latter (Cogan 1994: 37ff.). One author has argued that it is the use of entitlement programmes which should be made fully responsible for the deficit problem, since their percentage of the budget total grew from one third during the Eisenhower presidency to roughly two thirds in 1992 (Penner 1992: 139). Sturm has pointed to procedural change and a shift of 'organisational culture' in Congress for explaining the deficit problem (Sturm 1989: 259). Until the 1960s, members of appropriation committees had considered themselves as protectors of common-sense budgeting (respecting the principle of allowing as little debt as possible). Since then, this 'public regarding' attitude has lost importance, and another type of senator and representative has become predominant. Crudely put, this new type sees himself or herself more as a political entrepreneur whose foremost task is not to be a guardian of public spending.

Third, changes in Congress have been accompanied by the increase in frequency of the occurrence of a phenomenon called 'divided government', i.e. different party political affiliations of the President and one or two Chambers of Congress (Fiorina 1992: 6ff.). McCubbins, for example, argues that deficits occur when two different parties with different priorities simultaneously hold offices (McCubbins 1991: 83). Since the governmental system of checks and balances gives both branches a decisive vote in budgeting, gridlock is likely. A general aversion against tax increases in the United States worsens the situation. We will discuss the problem of gridlock in budgeting later. It should, however, be noted that there has been major criticism of this perspective of a general loss of budgetary control (Keech 1995; Roubini and Sachs 1989: 903ff.; Grilli 1991: 34ff.).

The major legal reforms intended to bring deficits under control and provide a remedy for this institutional failure (Budget Act of 1974, Gramm–Rudman–Hollings Act of 1985 and the Budget Enforcement Act of 1990) never succeeded in reforming the decision-making process in a way which would have produced better results, but simply added yet another level of decision-making to it (Shuman 1992:

211, 277, 304). In 1974 Congress tried to enable itself to produce its own budget proposal (White and Wildavsky 1989: 12ff.). It set up the Congressional Budget Office (CBO) and the Budget Committees as new actors in the budgetary process. The CBO was granted sufficient resources and know-how to provide Congress with the information necessary to formulate a 'counter-budget' to the presidential budget proposal. The budget committees were given the task of passing budget resolutions that define spending and revenue targets (ceilings) for the so-called budget functions. Other committees were supposed to operate independently and freely within this broad framework (White and Wildavsky 1989: 13ff.).

According to Tobin the new procedures worked fairly well until 1979 (Tobin 1979: 30). This suggestion has been challenged, however. Many scholars, among them White and Wildavsky, identified major weaknesses of the reform. These weaknesses, they argue, finally enabled President Ronald Reagan and Congress to expand deficit spending enormously during the 1980s (White and Wildavsky 1989: 16; Fisher 1985). Whether successful or not, the Reform Act of 1974 was an attempt both to centralise a decentralised decision-making process in Congress and to reduce some of the powers the President had been entrusted with by the 1921 Budget Act (Devins 1992: 66ff.). The 1974 reforms came about because of a unique alliance of Congressional left-wingers and fiscal conservatives in the post-Watergate political climate. The reform had wider aims than the improvement of budgetary policies (Penner 1992: 139). The relative loss of power of the President achieved in this reform was a political victory for Congress, and had less to do with a fresh start in budget-making. The institutional options provided for a balanced budget by the 1974 Act were never used. So the Act failed to cope efficiently with the budget problem (Gilmour 1990: 225). An alternative view could be that the 1974 Act was but a 'process reform' and was ultimately meant to be 'outcome neutral' (Joyce 1996: 318). In fact, it was the last major budget reform which had a broader approach to budgeting than just cutting back the deficit.

The Gramm–Rudman–Hollings Act (GRH 1985) (Balanced Budget and Emergency Deficit Control Act) was passed in 1985 (with an updated version after the Bowsher *v.* Synar decision of the Supreme Court in 1987). GRH constituted yet another attempt to improve the efficiency of budgeting by increasing its complexity. It added a further level of decision-making, 'sequestration', to the existing budgetary framework. The basic intention of the Act was to create a neutral institution, the General Accounting Office, with the ability to cut the budget automatically 'across the board' in case Congress and the President fail to remain with their budgets in the framework defined by deficit reduction limits. These limits, a 36 billion dollars reduction each year, would have made the federal goverment 'deficit-free' in a five-year period (Shuman 1992: 277ff.). Kate Stith characterised the reform act as follows (Stith 1988: 597):

> By establishing binding deficit limitations enforced outside of the legislative budget process, GRH sought to . . . amend our 'fiscal constitution', which for over two centuries had permitted prevailing legislative minorities to spend without limitation.

The attempt to 'de-politicise' the budgetary process (with respect to the deficit problem in particular) was successful for only a very short period, but never came even close to achieve the results originally intended. Still, GRH 1985 and its revised version of 1987 are landmark decisions, because they were attempts to create serious change. As Hanushek wrote (Hanushek 1986: 6), Gramm–Rudman–Hollings marked a switch from 'process rules' that only govern decisions, timing and priority setting to 'allocation rules', which specify budgetary results.

The official demise of GRH came when the Budget Enforcement Act in 1990 (BEA 1990) and the Omnibus Budget and Reconciliation Act of 1993 (OBRA 1993) established flexible deficit limits and the so-called Pay-As-You-Go-Rule (PAYGO). This rule requires immediate compensation for new expenditures by tax increases or spending cuts elsewhere in the budget (Davis and Keith 1995). The basic problem of budgeting, which is constituted by the separate decision-making processes on spending and taxation (or the financing of the budget) has never been dealt with seriously in the context of reforms (Hoover and Sheffrin 1992). It seems that not even the recent dramatic deficit problems in the late 1980s and 1990s have convinced Congress of the need to deal with the fragmentation and decentralisation of the budget process nor to reform its own internal decision-making structure, the committee system in particular. Recent reforms have focused attention on those activities of the government branches which Congress can actually control, i.e. spending and revenue raising, rather than on holding the President and Congress accountable for the annual deficit which is influenced by many other factors than the budget process as well (Joyce and Reischauer 1992).

Institutional arrangements seem to provide a good explanation for the growth of the budget and its causes. Institutions thus apparently matter, but so might ideas, too. A brief look at the justifications for fiscal and economic policy decisions since Roosevelt's New Deal brings to our attention that a new concept of what the state is and what it should do has evolved. Certainly, as mentioned before, Keynes was not the first person to integrate the government as an active variable into economic theory, thus giving it a crucial role in promoting economic welfare. Moreover, the states have always played an important role in shaping people's life, even at times when the federal government did not. Nonetheless, Keynes was indeed the first economist to define for government a permanent role in the economy. The state was supposed to counter-balance market forces, i.e. to substitute for a lack of demand by private actors in the economy. In this context, Keynes considered deficit spending as a legitimate instrument of economic policy-making, thus presenting a rationale for public deficits.

Although Keynes's theory became almost synonymous with Roosevelt's New Deal, this oversimplifies the interdependency of both approaches. Roosevelt did not refer to Keynes's ideas until 1937. He stuck to his 'balanced budget philosophy' till that date (Kimmel 1959: 178). Roosevelt apparently tried to legitimise his departure from his earlier budget philosophy by referring to other sets of economic ideas, such as the 'pump-priming theory' and the 'compensatory fiscal theory'. The latter essentially goes back to Kahn (Kahn 1931: 173ff.) and paved the way for Keynesian ideas. All of these approaches (though not all to the same extent) consider budgetary policies as a crucial factor for the performance of any given national economy.

It has been argued that Keynes's General Theory has simply served as an academic justification for what the government had (long) been doing (Hansen 1987:

52ff.). Governments had already taken responsibility in economic matters during the last third of the nineteenth century, but it was Keynes, so the argument goes, who delivered an economic rationale for their involvement. With Roosevelt the balanced budget philosophy did not, however, disappear. As Myrdal correctly stated (Myrdal 1990: xiv), 'In economics . . . all doctrines live on persistently. No new theories ever completely supplant the old.' What from our perspective is really new about the 'New Deal' is not necessarily the fact that budgetary policies became a tool of economic policies, but that the powerful balanced budget philosophy was now challenged by a powerful new economic philosophy, a rival who for a considerable period of time took over in the nation's capital. Roosevelt's successors in office continued to rely on Keynesian budgetary policies, e.g. by implementing additional automatic stabilisers in the fields of social and economic policies. Congress also adopted the Keynesian approach and passed laws, such as the Employment Act of 1946 (Kimmel 1959: 237, 281).

Deficit spending, initially considered as a kind of emergency cure, developed into a permanent and stable policy alternative to the seemingly out-dated balanced budget philosophy of the 1930s. Keynes did not really 'revolutionise' government policies, but he certainly provided a rationale for an approach to budgeting which had actually already been followed earlier. The balanced budget idea survived, however, at least as a symbol which the federal government apparently could not or did not want to give up. Institutional changes made it possible for the federal government to increase spending 'automatically'. Decentralisation in spending authority paved the way for the decentralisation of budgetary responsibility. Congress lost some of its powers to the President in 1921, but tried to regain them in 1974. Still no specific Congressional budgetary policy evolved, although pork-barrel spending[1] was a widespread Congressional phenomenon.

The institutional framework for decisions on the deficit

State deficits and the federal deficit

In the United States, federal and state powers are fairly clearly separated, especially in comparison with other federal countries, such as Germany. Thus, state deficits have little to do with federal deficits, at least as far as constitutional powers are concerned. Whereas the federal government has long been trying in vain to pass legislation on a constitutional limit to deficit growth, almost all states have such legislative hurdles. Some of these work better, some worse, some states have constitutional, some have purely legislative restrictions on their statute books (Lynch 1985: 17). None of the states has, however, succeeded in eliminating public debt. According to CRS data, the total gross debt of the states grew from $21.6 billion in 1962 to $315.5 billion in 1990 (Cox, Kiefer and Zimmerman 1994: 26).

With the enactment of balanced budget requirements, a shift in the balance of power between government branches on the state level occurred. For two reasons the power of the judiciary grew (Devins 1992: 78). On the one hand the deficit

Table 5.2 Legal restrictions on the state level

Year	Overall Property Tax rate limit	Specific Property Tax rate limit	Property Tax levy limit	General Revenue limit	General Expenditure limit	State limit	Type 1 Local Rate & Assess. Increase limit	Type 2 Rev., Expend. & Combined Rate & Assess. limit	Both Type 1 & Type 2 limits	State & Local Binding limit
1970	0	9	2	0	0	0	9	2	2	0
1971	0	9	3	1	2	0	9	5	3	0
1972	2	10	3	1	2	0	12	5	5	0
1973	2	13	4	1	4	0	14	7	5	0
1974	2	14	4	1	5	0	15	8	5	0
1975	2	14	4	1	5	0	15	8	5	0
1976	2	14	6	1	6	1	15	10	5	1
1977	2	14	6	1	6	3	15	10	5	2
1978	4	14	7	1	6	7	14	12	4	4
1979	4	14	9	1	6	13	13	14	5	7
1980	6	15	14	1	7	16	15	17	6	9
1981	6	15	15	1	7	17	15	18	6	9
1982	6	14	15	1	7	17	14	18	6	9
1983	6	14	16	1	7	17	14	19	7	10
1984	6	14	16	2	7	17	14	19	7	10
1985	6	14	17	2	7	18	14	20	7	11
1986	6	15	16	2	7	19	15	19	6	11
1987	6	15	17	2	7	19	15	20	7	12
1988	6	15	17	2	7	19	15	20	7	12
1989	6	13	17	2	7	19	13	20	5	12
1990	6	13	18	2	7	19	13	21	5	12

Source: Daniel R. Mullins and Philip G. Joyce, 'Tax and expenditure limitations and state and local fiscal structure: an empirical assessment', in: *Public Budgeting and Finance* 16(1) 1996, pp. 75–112, p. 80.

restrictions passed by state legislators gave room to judicial interpretation, on the other the courts' involvement became necessary to provide state governments with strategies for inventing around constitutional constraints. The minority vote in a report by the US Senate Committee on the Judiciary of 1995 lists some of the budgetary gimmicks used by state governments:

> These [dubious practices to disguise actual deficits] include shifting expenditures off budget; manipulating receipt and payment activities; accelerating tax revenues; postponing expenditures; delaying refunds to taxpayers and salaries to employees into a following fiscal year; reducing contributions to pensions funds by forcing changed actuarial assumption; and, borrowing repeatedly against the same assets by refinancing them after the original debt has been mostly repaid.
>
> (1995: 52)

Other techniques to avoid hard budgetary choices could be added, especially the creation of special districts, funds and agencies which basically now do the work the government used to do. The problems caused by outsourcing (state) borrowing to semi-public institutions were already identified by Walsh in the late 1970s (Walsh 1978). Semi-public borrowing is even further removed from voter control than deficits. It lacks democratic accountability, and, of course, is more expensive, since non-state debtors usually get less favourable interest rates than public borrowers (Fisher 1992: 91; Cox, Kiefer and Zimmerman 1994: 28). What is important to note from our perspective is that constitutional restrictions on budgeting as a means for improving the institutional framework for decisions on the deficit have not succeeded in eliminating deficits on the state level.

In many cases state governments have broader competences than the President of the United States (General Accounting Office 1993). Among these powers are the line-item veto and impoundment powers (rescissions and referrals) (Fisher 1992: 94ff.). We will deal with them later, since they play a role in recent discussions on the reform of budgetary procedures on the federal level, too. What should be noted here is that so far experience shows that these powers have contributed little to the reduction of the overall spending levels in the states (Carter and Schap 1990). It is also important to note that these powers were in part granted as the result of judicial rulings. The lesson to be learnt seems to be that more rigid budgetary constraints require a stronger executive branch. At least this is what the courts say. But the strengthening of the executive branch does not guarantee success. Still, reforms to reduce deficit spending always deprive legislators of some of their powers, on both the state and federal levels.

Federal budgeting

Budgeting on the federal level is a complex process. It has evolved over the centuries, was shaped by the separation of powers, and – according to most studies – is strongly influenced by the specific institutional framework which governs the budgetary process. This process is thus crucial for the development of the public debt.

First and foremost, the Constitution grants all budgetary powers to Congress. This means spending and revenue decisions need to be based on a legal foundation, i.e. a law. Not until the twentieth century did a budgetary process evolve. The executive, i.e. its various departments, would send in their requests and Congress would deal with them. In 1921 Congress passed the Budget and Accounting Act (Shuman 1992: 25ff.). From now on the executive was not only formally integrated into the budgetary process, because the President had to present his 'presidential budget' every year, but was also given a leading role in the budgetary process. The Act created the Bureau of the Budget which was placed in the Treasury Department in order to make the bureau's director directly answerable to the President. It was renamed Office of Management and Budgeting (OMB) in 1970 and was later even moved to the White House. What is so important about an institution that, in theory, simply monitors and supports budgetary decision-making in the executive? The answer is: information is crucial to budgeting. Presidents usually had budget directors they trusted completely. So over time the OMB became a central 'clearing house' for executive decision-making and an influential voice in the executive. The Act also created the General Accounting Office (GAO) as a congressional agency to review federal spending (Kettl 1992: 126). For the very first time in American history, Congress could now control the executive's spending practice.

Why did Congress lose budgetary power with the 1921 Act? The answer is simple: from now on the President set the agenda for federal budgeting. He presents a budget, the executive budget, which defines it. For Congress, a diversified body with hundreds of politicians following at least equally numerous and diverse interests, it is hard to present a powerful alternative that can rival the President's straightforward, unilateral policy decision on the plan for a budget.

With regard to the deficit it is important to note that the 1921 Act did not tackle one of the most crucial institutional deficiencies of the federal budgetary process: decisions on spending and revenues remained separate. As mentioned above, since the nineteenth-century spending decisions need both a legislative basis (authorisation) and an appropriation decision. This double requirement was later divorced, and the power of decision-making was spread over different Congressional committees. In other words, every spending decision needs to go through two decision-making processes at least. This procedural obstacle increases the number of decisions for which compromises have to be found. If the picture of a Congress with Congressmen and Congresswomen who seek to increase their share of the pie (to be transferred to their respective constituencies or campaign finance supporters) is correct, frequent decision-making gives rise to costly compromises and enhances pork-barrel spending. But this is just one aspect of the problem of budgetary consistency. Another one already mentioned is the fact that decisions on revenues are made separately from spending decisions. Spending decisions are prepared by 13 appropriations bills (the number corresponds to the number of appropriations subcommittees). Decisions on taxation and borrowing are prepared by different committees (i.e. the tax-writing committees) and approved in a separate vote in Congress.

From a lack of centralisation of budgetary decisions follows a lack of accountability for budgetary aggregates. This might help to explain the relative ease with which deficits were generated. The decision-making situation resembles a prisoner's dilemma: costs are spread over all actors, but gains are specified. Or to put it differently, the institutional framework encourages individual gain-seeking instead of enhancing collective responsibility. Phil Gramm, Congressman from Texas, has exemplified this decision-making logic as follows (White and Wildavsky 1989: 548):

> 'In the last Congress, the average bill we worked on with amendments cost about $50 million. There are 100 million taxpayers. That is 50 cents a head. The average beneficiary got $500. You do not have to have studied economics at Texas A&M (where he had taught) to know that somebody is willing to do more to get $500 than somebody is willing to do to prevent spending 50 cents.'
>
> (Addition in parentheses by White and Wildavsky.)

Moreover, as noted earlier, public borrowing is an easy way to avoid public resistance to certain policies. It avoids taxation by transferring costs to future budgets. The drawback is, however, that the immediate costs for public debts, the interests that have to be paid each year, make up an ever greater part of the annual budget.

Until 1974 the 1921 Act was only modestly revised. What explains the need for new legislation in 1974? As mentioned above, it is impossible to understand the 1974 Budget and Impoundment Control legislation, without looking at it in its historical context. One aspect here is the heightened public awareness of the deficit problem. Another aspect is the fact that President Nixon was under political pressure as a result of the Watergate investigation. Nixon's assertion of executive powers, especially his extensive and politically biased use of presidential impoundments, was no longer tolerated by Congress (Kettl 1992: 128). Congress felt that it was time for a radical change of policy and a change of direction in budgeting which would allow Congress to regain some of the powers it had so easily ceded to the executive. The 1974 Reform Act is just one of the examples which demonstrate Congressional loss of trust in the executive in the early 1970s.

What are the most important features of the 1974 Act? First of all, the annual budget process was confined to a strict time framework. Secondly, the President remained responsible for presenting his budget proposal to Congress. We can depict the budget process as prescribed by the 1974 Act as follows: the President sends in his budget proposal to Congress where it is distributed to all Congressional committees for assessment, i.e. for answering the question how the proposal might influence programmes that fall into the respective jurisdiction of a committee. The House and Senate Budget Committees then receive the other committees' 'Views and Estimates' of the budget by 15 March, and design a budget resolution. This budget resolution sets non-binding spending ceilings which are expected to guide Congress when it determines tax, authorisation and appropriations bills. In a way the Budget Committees manage Congressional counter-budgeting. The Budget Committees take into account the competing priorities outlined in the 'Views and Estimates' reports, testimony presented at hearings of the two budget committees, and economic estimates and programme analyses provided by the Congressional Budget Office (CBO) and the Joint Economic Committee of Congress.

After the proposed resolutions have been submitted to the House and Senate by the budget committees by 15 April (as laid down in the Act), both houses are required to approve some form of budget resolution by 15 May. The First Concurrent Budget Resolution then serves as a non-binding guide for all committees when considering their tax and spending bills. It indicates congressional fiscal priorities and assumptions on the state the nation's economy is in. This resolution is only an internal procedural device for Congress and not a law. It does not need presidential approval. With this First Resolution in hand, the congressional committees work to produce the relevant tax and authorisation legislation plus the above mentioned thirteen appropriations bills which actually allocate funds to government agencies and programmes. Before these bills take effect, the President must sign them into law.

The 1974 Act also provides for a Second Concurrent Budget Resolution. It seeks to institutionalise a procedural mechanism for spending restrictions. Unlike the first resolution, the second one is binding. But it still does not call for presidential approval. To enforce the Second Resolution, in the event that the appropriations bills exceed planned expenditures, Congress may include restrictive reconciliation language in the resolution. This language directs the relevant tax and spending committees to report legislation that would bring revenues and expenditures in line with the resolution (Savage 1990: 241).

In accordance with the Budget and Impoundment Control Act, the budget process should be completed by 1 October, the beginning of the new fiscal year. Budgetary timetables were, however, largely ignored by Congress. As can be observed up to the present day, continuing resolutions which extend funding levels from the preceding year are commonly employed to fund the government, because the necessary new legislation is still not in place. In addition, Second Resolutions have rarely been used; instead, First Resolutions have been made binding. This together with the instrument of reconciliation to iron out differences between the relevant committees involved in budgeting in Congress has become the major tool for radical policy change (as during the Reagan era) and thus has effectively 'centralised' part of the budgetary process (Joyce 1996: 319).

As mentioned above, some students of budgeting (Tobin 1979: 30) have argued that the 1974 Act worked fairly well throughout the 1970s. However, it could not cope with the rising deficit, especially during President Reagan's first term in office. The 1974 procedure lacked an effective enforcement mechanism. Thus, by 1985, Congress tried once again to find institutional arrangements for cutting back the deficit. The Gramm–Rudman–Hollings Act of 1985 (GRH 1985) added yet another procedure to the new institutional universe established by the Reform Act of 1974. First, it set up a deficit reduction plan which would have made the federal government 'deficit-free' within five years. Second, in case the government overspends its projected maximum deficit and if agreement between Congress and the President on where to cut spending or how to increase taxes cannot be reached, a new procedure, called sequestration, was planned to be initiated automatically. Under sequestration the General Accounting Office (GAO) would take responsibility and 'sequester', i.e. cut the budget across the board by the sum necessary to keep it within the planned deficit limit. The basic idea behind GRH 1985 was that it would be easier for a 'neutral' institution such as the GAO to take unpopular decisions and to cut back on all spending programmes than for any government branch headed by elected officials.

Ellwood called this strategy 'blame-avoidance behavior'. It provides politicians with the argument that 'the law made me do it'. In his opinion such a strategy cannot succeed (Ellwood 1988: 574):

the difficulty with expenditure limitations and balanced budget amendments is that they seek to cap the effects of politics rather than change the incentives that cause those effects.

Contrary to earlier assumptions the sequestration process was not completely neutral with regard to policy outcomes. Congress had built into sequestration a number of policy decisions. First and foremost, some expenditure programmes were exempted from the proposed cuts while others were subject only to limited cuts. Secondly, GRH required half the reductions to come from the defence budget. Thirdly – and the idea of 'neutrality' is implied here for the first time – the rest of the budget has to be cut by a uniform percentage (Gilmour 1990: 202).

The Supreme Court prevented the implementation of the first GRH Act. It argued that GRH was unconstitutional, because it violated the principle of separation of powers. An agency created by Congress, i.e. the GAO, should not be allowed to fulfill an executive task, i.e. to implement cut-backs in government spending (Bowsher *v.* Synar). Some scholars disagreed (Elliott 1987: 317ff.). They argued that a promising experiment had been stopped by a formalistic and unhelpfully narrow interpretation of the separation of powers doctrine. In 1987 GRH 1987 was passed. It contained new spending caps (i.e. a new deficit reduction plan) and now made the presidential OMB responsible for 'sequestration'. (By the way, Congress had already included a back-up provision in the 1985 GRH Act in the event that the Supreme Court would oppose the planned procedure.) Moving the enforcement mechanism to the politicised OMB was more than a technical change. The idea that the Presidential 'clearing-house' should have the power to sequester seemed frightening to Congressional Democrats. So they insisted on an amendment to the law which would give OMB little discretion with regard to how to cut the budget. Furthermore, Congress and the President 'watered down' the annual deficit targets, and postponed painfully tough decisions to the time after the 1988 presidential election (Kettl 1992: 97).

It was not until the Budget Enforcement Act (BEA 1990) and the Omnibus Budget Reconciliation Act (OBRA 1993) and its 'Pay-As-You-Go' Rule (PAYGO) were enacted that serious efforts were made to link spending and revenue-raising decisions. Each spending (or tax-cut) bill was now required to specify how losses of budgetary income were to be compensated either by raising revenue (tax increase) or by cut-backs in spending elsewhere. BEA 1990 eliminated the spending caps of GRH 1987 and replaced them by flexible spending limits. It aimed at identifying specific target amounts of annual savings, instead of trying to deal with the deficit itself (Eastaugh 1994: 5). BEA 1990 aggregated discretionary spending titles (see below) only for a short period from 1994 to 1995. It also provided for new legislation in 1995 which was to end PAYGO (OECD 1993: 51). OBRA 1993 saved, however, the global spending caps for discretionary expenditures and extended PAYGO until 1998. OBRA also broadened the tax base. It had the effect of a considerable increase of income tax for the well-to-do. The tax rate was raised by

5 per cent from 31 to 36 per cent, and a special levy on incomes above $250,000 was introduced which actually increases the tax rate to 39.6 per cent. These changes took effect retroactively on 1 January 1993, and were expected to provide the Internal Revenue Service with additional revenues of approximately 115 billion dollars (OECD 1993: 41). The OECD report also notes that the federal goverment's economic policy had not been a source for (new) deficits (OECD 1993: 33). The deficit problems were caused by mandatory spending, particularly on the health care system.

Mandatory spending programmes include open-ended entitlements and net interest expenses. The major transfer programmes are Social Security, Medicare and low-income assistance, federal employee pensions, deposit insurance, student loan subsidies, agricultural subsidies and net interest (OECD 1996a: 54). Discretionary spending includes nearly all purchases of goods and services, in particular compensation of active personnel. In addition, it covers many of the grants-in-aid (such as education and highways) and some transfer programmes (such as Pell grants for eduction) (OECD 1996a: ibid.). The 1990 and 1993 Reform Acts placed caps on discretionary spending programmes in order to limit spending aggregates and, as mentioned above, it introduced the PAYGO rule as a parliamentary hurdle to those decisions on tax and mandatory spending legislation which may increase the deficit (OECD 1996a: ibid.). Thus, there now exists an institutional reform of budgeting which has at least been partly successful in controlling the deficit. However, a new rigid institutionalised deficit control mechanism, such as 'sequestration' by a non-political agency, for example the GAO, seems unattainable in the near future thanks to the Bowsher *v.* Synar ruling. According to the OECD the merits of BEA 1990 and OBRA 1993 are as follows:

> Efforts have been made to reduce the federal budget deficit over the last decade. Progress has been uneven, but some success has been obtained. Indeed, the deficit looks set to decline for the fourth consecutive year in 1996; it will represent the smallest share of GDP since the mid-1970s and will be among the smallest in the OECD.
>
> (OECD 1996a: 52)

The OECD also mentions, however, that this success is not only due to institutional and policy improvements during the Bush and Clinton administrations, but also to an improving national economy which has been operating at roughly full employment over the past couple of years. Still, it is true to say that OBRA 1993, which also introduced hard freezes for discretionary spending and a deficit cut totalling 500 billion dollars until 1998 (OECD 1994), has had a positive impact on budgeting in general since its first year of full operation. However, old entitlement programmes have not been affected by PAYGO (Schick 1995). So, the biggest fiscal problem remains to be solved. In sum, PAYGO and other institutional changes have produced greater efficiency in deficit control policies, but the US Government still suffers from a constitutional arrangement that enhances stalemate and a decentralised budget process in Congress which makes it difficult to attribute responsibility for budgetary aggregates, including the deficit. Furthermore, the elimination of social (entitlement) programmes which create benefits for a large group of the electorate remains difficult in a democracy whose representatives have to pay attention to short-term election cycles. Still, with the Balanced Budget Act of 1997 a first effort was made. The Act reduced Medicare spending by 115 billion dollars over a five-year period.

Finally, a rather fundamental afterthought seems unavoidable. Where is the 'piece-meal reform' we have observed so far leading to? Budgeting in the United States has become a policy area which is governed by an illogical and unsystematic set of historically evolved rules which are understood by hardly anyone. Schick (1990: 169) once characterised congressional budgeting as 'saving the process by chang-ing it every year'. There is, however, some deeper concern connected with the consequences of institutional reform to combat the deficit than just a witty play with semantics. Fisher has argued (1985: 24):

> The power of the purse is not merely a means by which Congress controls the executive branch. It is also the way the public controls government. Any process that confuses legislators and the public, no matter how much it may delight the dreams of technicians, is too costly for a democracy.

The debt crisis in perspective

How do Americans feel about the deficit? The answer is more complicated than it seems at first sight. Of course, Americans are concerned, even distressed, if asked what they think about the growth of government debt during the 1980s and 1990s (Wirthlin Group 1995). After all, when President Jimmy Carter left the Oval Office, the United States had a gross national debt of about one trillion dollars. By 1996 it had virtually quadrupled. This growth resembles a mathematical function with exponential growth. The US Government needed almost 200 years (from 1789 to 1980) to accumulate one trillion dollars of public debt, but it added another three trillion in only roughly 15 years. As argued before, the problem of the debt is not necessarily its absolute figure (4 trillion dollars of public debt on the federal level), but its growth rate, which has started to accelerate earlier this century. What is important to note here is that the relative position of the United States among OECD countries has been improving for a couple of years. The deficit-to-GDP ratio has not only shrunk dramatically over time since the 1970s, but has also become one of the smallest in the OECD group (OECD 1996a: 52). Does this mean the deficit will cease to horrify the American people?

Looking at polls is one thing, but it is another to look at people's actual votes. In 1994, the Republicans clearly won the mid-term elections in both houses. The first legislative plan on their agenda was a Balanced Budget Constitutional Amendment (Müller 1997). House Joint Resolution 1 passed the House easily, but Senate Joint Resolution 1 failed by falling short of one vote. This did not end the debate, how-ever. In 1997, just after the 1996 elections, the Republicans tried again to introduce a Balanced Budget Amendment in Congress, but failed again. What is interesting is that there have been similar attempts since the 1930s, and moreover, they all have had some effect on budgeting and policy-making in general.

What do we know about the salience of the balanced budget issue? In opinion polls, the number of the interviewed supporting rigid measures against the deficit (such as a Balanced Budget Amendment) decreases immediately when asked whether as a consequence they would accept a personal disadvantage, say, a specific cut of spending for Medicaid, FADC or student loan grants. This is true for almost all social groups and many issue areas. People seem to support the abstract idea of a balanced budget, but they are not willing to accept its (personally) unpleasant consequences. Savage has presented a study which covers extensively the American history of balanced budgets and their ideological foundation (Savage 1990). He argues that 'balanced budgets' have long served as a symbol in American politics. They seem to be a constant and widespread factor, a phenomenon, of American political culture. As a real factor in politics, they often remained a myth. As mentioned above, all governments, before and after the American Revolution, have engaged in borrowing – in one form or another. All governments have also warned against the dangers of public deficits. Surprisingly enough, there has been little change over time with regard to the arguments brought forward by both the proponents and the critics of public borrowing. Among the most important issues of that discussion are three concerns (Müller 1998): ethical concerns, political concerns and economic concerns. Since all three are crucial for the debate on deficits in the United States, we will summarise them briefly here.

Ethical concerns are about the burden excessive spending today lays upon future generations. President Jefferson was among the first Americans using this argument to criticise public borrowing, and thus he may be regarded as the intellectual 'father' of a moralistic-conservative attitude towards deficits. It was a short logical step from Jefferson's concern to a call for limiting deficits in time. If the government of the day (and this implies the people) is convinced that public borrowing is necessary, then it should arrange for the repayment of the accumulated debt within the lifetime of one generation. While this argument may be plausible for consumption expenditures, it is illogical in the case of investments, for example expenditures on highways or railways. Requiring a government to adhere to strict time limits for the repayment of debts caused by spending on consumption is further complicated by the fact that not all public expenditures can easily be classified as consumption or investment expenditures, including most spending on social policies. Are schools an investment in the future or consumption? What about training programmes for the unemployed? Are subsidies for cultural activities just for the fun of audiences, or do they help maintain an infrastructure that is as important to any society as the highway system? It is even questionable whether the distinction between consumption and investment for public expenditures makes any sense at all. Whereas businesses can use the durability of any given expenditure as a crude yardstick for such a distinction, countries, states and local communities have a problem with determining the 'durable value' of any dollar spent. Spending, for example for social issues such as aid to families, low-income assistance or Medicaid, does not follow the logic of economic efficiency. The goal of such expenditure is neither the creation of profit nor of maximum shareholder value, but a politically determined social equilibrium that keeps society working. Thus, assigning costs and benefits to specific groups of people (generations) is a problematic approach, since it assumes the viability of the logic of property rights and of market fairness in this context.

Political and social concerns are also brought forward. The political argument in the tradition of the 'realist' school of thought in international relations is the following: growing deficits force the government to search for foreign capital investors who are ready to lend their money. Growing deficits, furthermore, increase the amount of interest payments on the debt. This in itself deepens a country's dependency on borrowed funds. Eventually, a point is reached where the government basically has no choice but to accept whatever conditions for additional borrowing foreign lenders will dictate. Payments on interests first reach economically dangerous levels, and finally even political demands will be brought forward by foreign capital owners. Pessimists see the administration in Washington DC already today as a puppet on the string of Asian and European capital investors.

The actual situation is less spectacular and contradicts such conspiracy theories. First and foremost, for decades the share of foreign lending as part of the gross national debt has remained constantly at a level of about 20 per cent. In other words, the enormous increase in government debt over the past 15 years or so was not primarily financed by foreign investors. There is no significant sign that this will soon change dramatically. For obvious reasons more continuity is to be expected. US Government bonds are still a risk-free investment. They therefore remain attractive to domestic institutional investors, such as banks, insurance companies or money market funds, as well as to the government itself. Social Security, the Federal Reserve and state and local governments hold large percentages (together over 50 per cent) of the federal debt (Kettl 1992: 27). However, the absolute quantity of foreign lending has risen. What, some critics may argue, if 20 per cent is in fact sufficient to permit meaningful pressure upon the US Government? A reply to this question could be: what kind of pressure? After all, the US dollar is a government monopoly. Thus, the currency held by foreign investors can be wholly re-regulated, devalued and even destroyed by the federal government. In any worst-case scenario Washington's power is definitely stronger than any potential threat by foreign lenders.

If the fear of foreign investors' power may count as the 'realist' version of political concerns caused by the size of the public debt, the social concerns are its 'liberal' version. Central to these concerns is the fact that a rising burden of interests narrows the room for manoeuvre in budgeting. It is indeed the case that interest payments on the national debt have meanwhile become one of the biggest items of the federal budget. A number of economic concerns have been voiced in addition. Deficits were made responsible for all kinds of economic ills, including higher interest rates, higher inflation or even negative effects for the exchange rate of the US dollar.

Savage rendered great service to the study of public deficits by systematically comparing empirical data for the United States with different theoretical propositions brought forward by advocates of balanced budgets (Savage 1990: 9ff.). Unfortunately, his data material ends in 1984. His results are, however, clear: there is little proof of a significant, constant and reliable correlation between public deficits and any major macro-economic indicator. The choice of time periods, of variables to test and finally the methodological mix strongly determine the results of any empirical study in that field. Of course, there have been studies which found correlations between different indicators (Cagan 1985; Feldstein and Eckstein 1970). Other contributions have, however, either negated these findings or found different correlations with a similar research designs, but using other data (Müller 1997). The concrete impact of public deficits on a national economy depends on the specific condition an economy is in. Deficit spending has been used as a policy tool for supporting economic recovery since the life-time of John Maynard Keynes. Empirical data are, however, not unambiguous here, not even for the well-researched case of the United States. What is interesting is the continuing debate between the proponents of the Keynesian approch ('governments should balance the economy, not simply the budget') (Saturno 1994: 2) and the proponents of the neoliberal–monetarist 'small government' philosophy. To put it more precisely, the diametrically opposed attitudes towards (balanced) budgets do not always result from different approaches to sound public finance. They have a lot more to do with different conceptions of the state and its role in the national economy. The American debate on the pros and cons of balanced budgets has been a fight over the competences of governments (federal and state) in general and the role of government in the economy in particular. Sound public finance in a technical sense has always been a problem of the second order. Higher taxes have never really been an alternative to deficits. Proponents of balanced budgets are usually also inclined to favour tax cuts. On the other hand, optimists, such as Tobin and others, who do not see that deficits create much harm, are usually also less critical of high levels of taxation.

Deficit control policies

As demonstrated above, the policies of institutional change in budgetary procedures have increasingly become identical with deficit control policies. Whilst the first Act which institutionalised the budget process, the Budget and Accounting Act of 1921, had other intentions as well, the following major reform efforts, such as the 1974, 1985, 1987, 1990 and 1993 legislation, were largely, if not totally, a reaction to concerns about the financial situation of the federal government.

Beside such attempts at institutional reform, there have been other efforts to cope with the deficit. One of these was President Reagan's tax reform of 1981 which basically endorsed the supply-siders' view that tax cuts lead to a strengthening of the economy, thus to higher (absolute) tax revenues and as a result to smaller deficits (Shuman 1992: 249). There have also been attempts at rational budgeting, especially during the Carter era. The idea of a professionalised executive which follows the rationale of 'good', business-like management rather than the inconclusive signals of politics dates back as early as the Wilson presidency (Kimmel 1959: 87; Koven 1988: 168). It re-appeared in the 1960s and 1970s, as a re-born manifestation of rationalisation which fitted the 'planning euphoria' then in vogue. It took the form of Performance Budgeting, Planning-Programming-Budgeting System

(PPBS), Management by Objectives (MBO) and Zero-Base Budgeting (ZBB) and the like (Wilson 1980; Kettl 1992: 68–91). Not unlike the story of Reagan's tax cut, in this case theory was betrayed by reality. President Reagan did not collect additional tax income, and President Carter could not make his budget proposals 'more rational'. Today 'rational' approaches to budgeting are considered to have failed in practical terms. Nowhere have they controlled deficits efficiently. Latest developments with regard to rational budgeting on the policy level, such as the reform of the Social Security system (OECD 1995: 95ff.), try to concentrate their attention on specific costly spending items and try to re-arrange them in a way which makes budget cuts more effective.

Recently three major efforts have been made to control deficits by institutional innovation. First, legislation to alter the institutional framework for budgetary decision-making was debated. Among the most important efforts here are the above-mentioned reform acts. Secondly, separate legislative action was initiated which concerns (constitutional) powers broader than those relevant to budgeting. An example recently debated and codified by legislation is the so-called line-item veto. Thirdly, for a long time attempts have been made to change the constitutional framework of budgeting itself. A regular feature of this debate has been the idea of a Balanced Budget Amendment to the Constitution. We will devote the rest of this chapter to the description and explanation of the basic ideas inherent in these approaches.[2]

We have already discussed the effects of the 1974 reforms of the budgetary process and more recent legislation. Changes made here tightened up the budgetary process. They have introduced new mechanisms of decision-making, such as sequestration or PAYGO, and have tried to increase the probability of expenditure cuts (e.g. by aggregating spending items). However, with regard to entitlements and other direct spending, PAYGO only requires any increases here to be offset by reductions elsewhere or by higher revenues. It does nothing to control effectively established programmes and expenditure increases required by law (Schick 1995: 127). Furthermore, reforms of budgetary procedures have never tried to reform Congress's internal decision-making procedures. In this respect, all reform efforts remained on the surface of the problem, no matter how well planned and well intentioned some of them were. It should, however, be noted that Congress has learnt its lesson. As mentioned earlier, the focus of reform efforts has moved from establishing a process (1974) and controlling the deficit (1985), to controlling spending (1990, 1993 and 1997).

Butler has argued that the privatisation of federal services can both reduce the budget total and create coalitions of interest groups dedicated to maintaining and expanding privatisation (Butler 1987: 266ff.). What he assumes is that goverment ought to become a 'facilitator', rather than a provider, of goods and services for society (Butler 1987: 268). As an example for this deflection of demand for services from the public to the non-governmental sector by the use of incentives, he cites the case of IRAs (Individual Retirement Accounts) and Social Security (Butler 1987: 269):

> Almost as an afterthought, however, Congress attached a provision to the 1981 tax act, allowing all working Americans to open tax deductible IRAs. In so doing, Congress

planted the seeds of a private Social Security alternative. It was not long before the political dynamics of privatization began to be felt. Even before the new law went into effect, banks and other financial institutions began a massive campaign to encourage the public to open IRAs. The privatization coalition was born. . . . When the legislation was before Congress, Treasury estimates put the 1982 cost of the deduction at about $3,000,000,000; it turned out to be nearer to $10,000,000,000.

Although the 'Reinventing Government' movement has taken up this idea and, furthermore, although the new debate on the 'regulatory state' has been stimulated not least by the tightening of national budgets, budgetary reform proposals have usually taken another direction.

Secondly, the line-item veto has been part of the debate on budgetary reform for a long time. It reappeared after the mid-term election of 1994. It was part of the general strategy of Republicans to cope with the deficit, but in Congress it was also supported by Democrats. The version of the line-item veto finally enacted in 1996 enhanced the President's rescission authority from 1997 onwards at first only for an eight-year period. This meant that the presidential veto, as laid down in the constitution, were to be extended to the power to 'cancel in whole any dollar amount of discretionary budget authority provided in an appropriation law or any item of new direct spending or limited tax benefit contained in any law' (Joyce and Reischauer 1997: 97). Although it is dubious if any legislation can bind Congress forever, the line-item veto seemed to have good chances for survival and could have become an important new instrument of budgetary control if existing expenditure controls are weakened. To effectively overrule the President or to eliminate the line-item veto from a given piece of legislation, Congress would have had to pass a new bill; this could, of course, in turn be vetoed by the President, since Congress can definitely not exclude the President's constitutional right to veto any bill as a whole. To overrule the (standard) presidential veto, Congress would have to find a two-third majority in both houses.

The line-item veto raises, however, a number of practical questions with regard to American constitutionalism in general and American constitutional governance in particular. We have already mentioned that state experience suggests that enhanced rescission powers of the executive do not guarantee reduced spending levels. Several studies have argued that a number of effects of the line-item veto on the state level are less than desirable (Burkhead 1956), and that some of these effects are likely to reappear on the federal level as well (Lauth 1996). After all, the 'real' problem, the existing level of direct spending (through entitlements), is not a part of annual appropriation laws, and thus it is not subject to the line-item veto. New expenditure programmes may be vetoed by the President, but there is already specific legislation to control them. This is why Joyce and Reischauer (1997: 100) saw little immediate effect of the line-item veto:

Discretionary spending is already fairly strictly controlled by the spending caps that were established under the Budget Enforcement Act of 1990 (BEA) and, more recently, by lower limits etablished in the Congressional Budget Resolutions. Substantial expansions of direct spending authority or limited tax benefits do not seem likely, given the narrow definition used in the law, with or without the item veto. The PAYGO discipline has effectively curtailed such legislation.

As could be predicted, the line-item veto, once it was used, was challenged before the courts. New York City Council and the Snake River Potato Growers of Idaho, both affected by the President's line-item veto in two different pieces of legislation, brought their cases to the Supreme Court. In June 1998 the Court struck down the line-item veto by a 6–3 vote. It argued that the veto gave the President what amounted to legislative authority, because he was able to change the text of duly enacted statutes. This violated the constitutional principle of separation of powers. The American President lost in this way a very handy tool for controlling spending and for weeding out legislation he did not like. Since he was given the line-item veto President Clinton had used it 82 times to cut more than $300 million from bills. To save the line-item veto a constitutional amendment would now be necessary. It is, however, highly unlikely that the initiative for such an amendment will be taken soon.

In 1798 Jefferson wrote to his friend John Taylor (Savage 1990: 2):

> I wish it were possible tq obtain a single amendment to our constitution. I would
> be willing to depend on that alone for the reduction of the administration of our
> government to the genuine principles of its constitution: I mean an additional article,
> taking from the federal government the power of borrowing.

As a reaction to the New Deal policy of Roosevelt, Representative Harold Knutson introduced House Joint Resolution 579 in 1936, but he failed to mobilise the necessary majorities. Knutson proposed a constitutional amendment which would have basically been true to Jefferson's idea. Knutson was the first politician to bring this idea to Congress, but he was certainly not the last one. He was succeeded by numerous other advocates of constitutional reform. This debate did not, however, attract a high level of public attention, until New Jersey became the first state to pass legislation to control state spending and the deficit in 1976 (Cebula 1987: 62). Other states followed soon, and as of now virtually all states have introduced some form of restriction to public borrowing. However, as Mullins and Joyce have argued, these 'tax and expenditure limitations' (TELs) led to mixed results. Their most important effects concerned more the composition of state (and local community) budgets than their absolute size – including the size of the deficit (Mullins and Joyce 1996). On the federal level, six attempts to pass a constitutional balanced budget amendment failed: in 1982, 1986, 1990, 1992, 1995 and 1997 (Dauster 1992: 15; Müller 1997). They failed at different stages of the legislative process and with different voting records. The 1995 effort has so far been the one closest to success. Whether any of these efforts would have had a chance to make it through three-fourths of all states (usually the state legislatures) is yet another question. The high and ever higher level of support for a balanced budget amendment to the US Constitution, however, implies that it is potentially a powerful weapon in the fight against the deficit. We will survey its various aspects briefly.

There have been different proposals for the details of a balanced budget amendment. The most prominent proposals are the so-called tax-expenditure limitation and the balanced budget requirement. Whilst the latter simply requires the government to balance the budget and, in its most extreme form, does not care about the level of government spending as long as enough tax revenues are raised to finance it, the first approach concentrates on the level of government activity. To give an example, the following summarises major provisions of the 1995 proposal (Saturno 1995: 3):

(1) total outlays must not exceed receipts, unless a deficit is allowed by a three-fifths rollcall vote in each House (261 Members in the House and 60 Members in the Senate);

(2) the limit on debt held by the public can only be raised by a three-fifths rollcall vote in each House;

(3) the President must submit a budget reflecting a budgetary balance;

(4) no bill to increase revenue can become law unless approved by an absolute majority vote in each House (218 Members in the House and 51 Members in the Senate);

(5) the requirements may be waived only in the event of a declared war or declared imminent and serious military threat;

(6) all receipts (except borrowing) and all outlays (except for the repayment of debt principal) are covered;

(7) Congress must enforce the Article by appropriate legislation;

(8) The effective date of this provision is FY 2002 or the second year after ratification, whichever is later.

This proposal has a number of interesting features. First, it does not discriminate between different kinds of expenditures, i.e. consumption and investment, not even between mandatory spending and discretionary spending. Other proposals exclude, for example, Social Security from spending limits. Secondly, it does not refer to the role of the judiciary and to the question what happens if Congress does not adhere to these provisions. Thirdly, and most important in terms of 'ideological budgeting', this is a government limitation act rather than a balanced budget provision. As a proposal for constitutional reform it implies a 'small government' philosophy. It is not about sound finance, it is about the role of the state. This latter point may be the most questionable aspect of this kind of constitutional reform.

President Clinton and the 105th Congress are still committed to the aim of balancing the budget until the year 2002 – with or without a constitutional amendment. Thanks to 'sounder' fiscal policies of both branches of Congress and good economic conditions, the deficit has been shrinking now for a couple of years. In 1998 President Clinton presented Congress with a proposal for the nation's first balanced budget in 30 years. The plan is to balance the budget for the 1999 fiscal year which begins in October 1998. The irony of history may be that a balanced budget can become reality more easily than a constitutional amendment which was intended to force politicians to work for this very end.

Deficits – the United States experience

It is typical for the way the deficit problem was handled in the United States that deficits have always been the symptom of more than an economic problem. Very early in the nation's history political positions on the deficit were closely connected with much more general views on the role of the state in society on the one hand and institutional questions on the other. The most important institutional question concerned and still concerns the relationship between the President and Congress, but also the ability of Congress to make budgets.

Due to the size of the public debt and the popularity of anti-statist economic philosophies since the 1980s, during the last two decades the deficit came increasingly to be seen also as a problem in its own right and as such was able to dominate the domestic political agenda to the extent that other policy decisions were made dependent on the success of deficit control policies. This is, by the way, also how decision-makers themselves began to feel. Robert Reich (1997: 63), President Clinton's then Secretary of Labor, for example, almost desperately reported from a Cabinet meeting on 13 February 1993: 'Deficit, deficit, deficit, deficit, deficit. We have to cut it. By how much? That's all we talk about in the Roosevelt Room.'

The problem that emerged already in the 1970s was that although it was easy to find a general consensus on the need to reduce annual deficits, concrete decisions to this end were often blocked either in Congress or because of a conflict between Congress and the President. The procedural complexities of the budgetary process in Congress gave even small groups of Representatives a good chance to take parts of the budgetary process hostage in order to succeed with their political and financial demands. This provoked the search for 'neutral' devices which would automatically cut or rule out deficits, such as a balanced budget amendment to the Constitution or a procedure to force Congress to gradually bring about a balanced budget. It soon turned out that politics left no room for a 'neutral' budgetary decision-making process. As the political consensus in the United States ruled out a strategy of tax increases to secure additional revenues to balance the budget, deficit control policies had to concentrate on the control of government spending. This moved the issue back into the field of political controversy. Old questions were asked with new urgency as, for example, should defence expenditures be cut, or what could be done about social expenditures which make up a huge part of government expenditures? Deficit control policies began to have very immediate political and above all social consequences.

The economic success of the late 1990s, some modest tax increases of the Bush presidency and rigorous spending cuts, which affect above all lower incomes, enabled the United States to find at least temporarily a solution for the deficit problem. A balanced budget was no longer impossible. But this does not solve the underlying debt problem. Public debt accumulated over time does not disappear overnight. In 1996 it was still 50 per cent of GDP. The OECD (1997: 58) has calculated that even assuming a balanced budget for the years 2002–7, without additional measures to deal with the long-term problems of Medicare, Medicaid and Social Security the ratio of debt to GDP reaches 283 per cent in 2050. Metaphorically speaking, the debt monster may have fallen asleep, but if it is not attacked again and again, it will wake up and come back to cause trouble.

Notes

1. Spending on pet projects of Congressmen and Congresswomen which are of special benefit to their districts and to their campaigns for re-election.
2. These and further proposals are also discussed in Schick 1995: 197–203.

References

Anderson, Gary M. (1987) 'The US federal deficit and national debt: a political and economic history', in: Buchanan, James M., Rowley, Charles K. and Tollison, Robert D. (eds), *Deficits*, New York: Blackwell, pp. 9–46.

Barro, Robert J. (1986) 'U.S. deficits since World War I', in: *Scandinavian Journal of Economics* 88, pp. 195–222.

Buck, Arthur E. (1929) *Public Budgeting*, New York: Harper & Bros.

Burdekin, Richard Charles K. and Langdana, Farrokh K. (1992) *Budget Deficits and Economic Performance*, London and New York: Routledge.

Burkhead, Jesse (1956) *Government Budgeting*, New York: John Wiley.

Butler, Stuart M. (1987) 'Privatization: the antidote to budget-cutting failures', in: Fink, Richard H. and High, Jack C. (eds), *A Nation in Debt: Economists Debate the Federal Budget Deficit*, Frederick: University Publications of America, pp. 266–71.

Cagan, Phillip (1985) *The Economy in Deficit*, Washington, D.C.: American Enterprise Institute.

Carter, John R. and Schap, David (1990) 'Line-item veto: where is thy sting?', in: *Journal of Economic Perspectives* 4(2) (Spring), pp. 103–18.

Cebula, Richard J. (1987) *The Deficit Problem in Perspective*, Lexington and Toronto: Lexington Books.

Cogan, John F. (1994) 'The dispersion of spending authority and federal budget deficits', in: Cogan, John F., Muris, Timothy and Schick, Allen (eds), *The Budget Puzzle. Understanding Federal Spending*, Stanford: Stanford University Press, pp. 16–40.

Cooke, Jacob E. (ed.) (1964) *The Reports of Alexander Hamilton*. New York: Scribner's.

Cox, William A., Kiefer, Donald W. and Zimmerman, Dennis (1994) *A Balanced Budget Constitutional Amendment: Economic Issues*, CRS Report for Congress, Washington, D.C.: CRS.

Croly, Herbert (1909) *The Promise of American Life*, New York: Macmillan.

Dauster, William G. (1992) 'Budget process issues for 1993', in: *Journal of Law and Politics* 9, pp. 9–38.

Davis, Edward and Keith, Robert (1995) *Budget Enforcement Procedures: Application to Social Security Revenues and Spending*, CRS Report for Congress (95-255 GOV), Washington, D.C.: CRS.

Devins, Neal (1992) 'A symbolic balanced budget amendment', in: *Journal of Law and Politics* 9, pp. 61–88.

Eastaugh, Steven R. (1994) *Facing Tough Choices. Balancing Fiscal and Social Deficits*, Westport: Praeger.

Elliott, E. Donald (1987) 'Regulating the deficit after Bowsher v. Synar', in: *Yale Journal on Regulation* 4, pp. 317–61.

Ellwood, John (1988) 'The politics of the enactment and implementation of Gramm–Rudman–Hollings: why Congress cannot address the deficit dilemma', in: *Harvard Journal on Legislation* 25, pp. 553–75.

Feldstein, Martin and Eckstein, Otto (1970) 'The fundamental determinants of the interest rate', in: *Review of Economics and Statistics* 52, pp. 363–75.

Fink, Richard H. and High, J.C. (eds) (1987) *A Nation in Debt: Economists Debate the Federal Budget Deficit*, Frederick: University Publications of America.

Fiorina, Morris P. (1992) *Divided Government*, New York: Macmillan.

Fisher, Louis (1985) 'Ten years of the Budget Act: still searching for controls', in: *Public Budgeting and Finance* 5 (1985), pp. 3–28.

Fisher, Louis (1992) 'The effects of a balanced budget amendment on political institutions', in: *Journal of Law and Politics* 9, pp. 89–104.

General Accounting Office (1993) *Balanced Budget Requirements: State Experiences and Implications for the Federal Government*, GAO/AFMD-95-58BR, Washington, D.C.: GAO.

Gilmour, John B. (1990) *Reconcilable Differences? Congress, the Budget Process and the Deficit*, Berkeley: University of California Press.

Grilli, Vittorio *et al.* (1991) 'Institutions and policies', in: *Economic Policy* 13, pp. 341–92.

Hansen, Alvin (1987) 'Fiscal policy. New and old, in: Fink, Richard H. and High, J.C., *A Nation in Debt. Economists Debate the Federal Deficit*, Frederick: University Publications of America, pp. 52–7.

Hanushek, Eric (1986) 'Formula budgeting: the economics and analytics of fiscal policy under rules. in: *Journal of Policy Analysis and Management* 6, pp. 3–19.

Hoover, Kevin V. and Sheffrin, Steven M. (1992) 'Causation, spending, and taxes: sand in the sandbox or tax collector for the welfare state', in: *American Economic Review* 82, pp. 225–48.

Ippolito, Dennis S. (1990) *Uncertain Legacies. Federal Budget Policy from Roosevelt through Reagan*, Charlottesville and London: University Press of Virginia.

Joyce, Philip G. (1996) 'Congressional budget reform: the unanticipated implications for federal policy making', in: *Public Administration Review* 56, pp. 317–25.

Joyce, Philip G. and Reischauer, Robert D. (1992) 'Deficit budgeting: the federal budget process and budget reform', in: *Harvard Journal on Legislation* 29, pp. 429–53.

Joyce, Philip G. and Reischauer, Robert D. (1997) 'The federal line item-veto: what is it and what will it do?', in: *Public Administration Review* 57, pp. 95–104.

Kahn, Richard F. (1931) 'The relation of home investment to unemployment', in: *Economic Journal* 41, pp. 173–98.

Keech, William R. (1995) *Economic Politics. The Costs of Democracy*, Cambridge: Cambridge University Press.

Keller, Morton (1977) *Affairs of State: Public Life in Late Nineteenth-Century America*, Cambridge (Mass.): Harvard University Press.

Kettl, Donald F. (1992) *Deficit Politics. Public Budgeting in Its Institutional and Historical Context*, New York: Macmillan.

Kimmel, Lewis H. (1959) *Federal Budget and Fiscal Policy 1789–1958*, Washington, D.C.: Brookings Institution.

Koven, Steven G. (1988) *Ideological Budgeting. The Influence of Political Philosophy on Public Policy*, New York/Westport and London: Praeger.

Lauth, Thomas (1996) 'The line-item veto in government budgeting, in: *Public Budgeting and Finance* 16, pp. 97–112.

Lynch, Thomas D. (1985) *Public Budgeting in America*, Englewood Cliffs: Prentice-Hall.

McCraw, Thomas K. (1984) *Prophets of Regulation*, Cambridge (Mass.): Harvard University Press.

McCubbins, Mathew D. (1991) 'Party governance and U.S. budget deficits: divided government and fiscal stalemate', in: Alesina, Alberto and Carliner, Geoffrey (eds), *Economics and Politics in the Eighties*, Chicago: University of Chicago Press, pp. 83–112.

Malone, Dumas (1951) *Jefferson and His Time: Jefferson and the Rights of Man*, vol. 2, Boston: Little.

Müller, Markus M. (1997) *Haushaltsausgleich durch Verfassungspolitik? Ein Beitrag zur Diskussion um ein Balanced Budget Amendment in den USA*, Berlin: Logos.

Müller, Markus M. (1998) *Staatsverschuldung, in: Staatsbürger- und Parlamentslexikon*, München: Oldenbourg, pp. 863–4.

Mullins, Daniel R. and Joyce, Philip G. (1996) 'Tax and expenditure limitations and state and local fiscal structure: an empirical assessment', in: *Public Budgeting and Finance* 16, pp. 75–112.

Myers, Margaret G. (1970) *A Financial History of the U.S.*, New York: Columbia University Press.

Myrdal, Gunnar (1990) *The Political Element in the Development of Economic Theory*, Brunswick: Transaction.

OECD (1993) *Wirtschaftsberichte. Vereinigte Staaten*, Paris: OECD.

OECD (1994) *Wirtschaftsberichte. Vereinigte Staaten*, Paris: OECD.

OECD (1995) *Wirtschaftsberichte. Vereinigte Staaten*, Paris: OECD.

OECD (1996) *Managing Structural Deficit Reduction*, Public Management Occasional Papers No. 11, Paris: OECD.

OECD (1996a) *Economic Surveys: United States*, Paris: OECD.

OECD (1997) *Economic Surveys: United States*, Paris: OECD.

Penner, Rudolph G. (1992) 'The budget deficit: political monster born of political pets', in: *Journal of Law and Politics* 9, pp. 137–45.

Rabushka, Alvin (1988) 'A constitutional cure for deficits', in: Meyer, Lawrence H. (ed.), *The Economic Consequences of Government Deficits*, Boston, Den Haag, Dordrecht and Lancester: Kluwer, pp. 183–99.

Regalia, Martin (1995) 'Testimony before the Senate Judiciary Committee during January 5, 1995 Hearings on a balanced budget constitutional amendment', in: *Congressional Digest* 74(2), p. 54.

Reich, Robert (1997) *Locked in the Cabinet*, New York: Alfred A. Knopf.

Rossiter, Clinton (1961) *The Federalist Papers: Alexander Hamilton, James Madison, John Jay*, with an introduction, table of contents, and index of ideas by Clinton Rossiter, New York: New American Library.

Roubini, Nouriel and Sachs, Jeffrey D. (1989) 'Political and economic determinants of budget deficits in the industrial democracies', in: *European Economic Review* 33, pp. 903–33.

Saturno, James V. (1994) *A Balanced Budget Constitutional Amendment: Background and Congressional Options*, CRS Report for Congress, Washington, D.C.: CRS.

Saturno, James V. (1995) *A Balanced Budget Constitutional Amendment: Procedural Issues*, Washington D.C.: CRS.

Savage, James D. (1990) *Balanced Budgets and American Politics*, Ithaca and London: Cornell University Press.

Savage, James D. (1992) 'Thomas Jefferson's Balanced Budget Amendment: an introduction to the Symposium on the Federal Budget', in: *Journal of Law and Politics* 9, pp. 2–9.

Schick, Allen (1990) *The Capacity to Budget*, Washington, D.C.: The Urban Institute Press.

Schick, Allen (1995) *The Federal Budget. Politics, Policy, Process*, Washington, D.C.: The Brookings Institution.

Senate Committee on the Judiciary (1995) *Balanced-Budget Constitutional Amendment. Report together with Additonal, Minority, and Supplemental Views* (Report 104–5), Washington, D.C.

Shuman, Howard E. (1992) *Politics and the Budget. The Struggle Between the President and the Congress*, Englewood Cliffs: Prentice Hall.

Stith, Kate (1988) 'Rewriting the fiscal constitution: the case of Gramm–Rudman–Hollings, in: *California Law Review* 76, pp. 593–668.

Sturm, Roland (1989) *Haushaltspolitik in westlichen Demokratien. Ein Vergleich des haushaltspolitischen Entscheidungsprozesses in der Bundesrepublik Deutschland, Frankreich, Großbritannien, Kanada und den USA*, Baden-Baden: Nomos.

Tobin, James (1979) 'The federal budget and the constitution. A constitutional blunder is a bigger mistake than deficit financing', in: *Taxing and Spending* 2, pp. 30–42.

Walsh, Annemarie H. (1978) *The Politics and Practices of Government Corporations*, Cambridge (Mass.): MIT Press.

White, Joseph and Wildavsky, Aaron (1989) *The Deficit and the Public Interest. The Search for Responsible Budgeting in the 1980s*, Berkeley: University of California Press.

Wilson, David E. (1980) *The National Planning Idea in U.S. Public Policy: Five Alternative Approaches*, Boulder: Westview Press.

Wirthlin Group (1995) *A National Survey Measuring Sentiment Towards the Balanced Budget Amendment*, Washington, D.C.: Wirthlin Group.

Chapter 6

Public deficits: a challenge to governance?

A prominent American political scientist recently remarked (Peters 1991: 105):

> An unbalanced budget has been blamed for almost all the ills of humankind except
> fallen arches. At a personal level, Charles Dickens' Mr Micawber provided a simple
> test for personal happiness based on the balanced budget. At the national level, the
> decline of nations and the fall of empires has been attributed to financial profligacy.

We have seen that the history of the development of the public debt in the four
nations studied here is less dramatic than the above suggests. However, although
there is no reason for being too pessimistic, it would also be wrong to sit back and
expect the phenomenon of public deficits and the incredible degree of indebtedness
resulting from the history of unbalanced budgets to disappear overnight by some
mysterious economic stroke of luck. The most worrying aspect of public deficits
seems to be that we have difficulties in understanding their importance for our daily
lives. Experts evaluate them by some broad notions of economic performance,
based on economic models and theories. Though theories have reached a high
degree of formal elegance, they by no means produce unanimous judgements on
the nature of present situations, nor do they help us make clear strategic choices
with regard to policy-making. Theoretical advice has also done little to guide the
behaviour of politicians and to improve their understanding of social consequences
of deficits and economics in general. Deficits are helpful to straighten the business
cycle and to avoid economic crises: for politicians this was clearly the lesson of the
decades of Keynesianism. Today's message seems to be that nations should balance
their budgets and reduce their overall indebtedness. The latter is the more complicated task, because even under conditions of modest economic growth (which is
nowhere guaranteed) it implies a reduction of living standards today with the intention of putting one's house in order for the coming generations.

Table 6.1 shows that the indebtedness of the four nations studied here did not
evolve in parallel. Still, the oil shock of 1973–4 was a kind of watershed in deficit
policies. Successful models of earlier crisis management, such as the various public
spending efforts in the New Deal era, which, as some economists have argued, have
helped to overcome the consequences of the world economic crisis of the early

Table 6.1 A comparison of government indebtedness/gross financial liabilities*
as a percentage of nominal GNP/GDP**

	1970	1975	1980	1985	1990	1995
United States	46.2	44.7	37.0	49.5	55.5	63.4
Germany	18.4	24.9	31.1	42.8	45.5	62.2
United Kingdom	86.2	65.0	54.0	58.9	39.3	60.0
Canada	53.7	44.7	44.0	64.1	72.5	100.5

* Government indebtedness (total) for 1970–5; general government gross
financial liabilities, as defined below, for 1980–95. General government gross
financial liabilities include all financial liabilities as defined by the system of
National Accounts (where data permits) and covers the general government
sector, which is a consolidation of central government, state and local
government and the social security sector.
** nominal GNP for 1970–5; nominal GDP for 1980–95.
Sources: OECD.

1930s, lost credibility. Keynesian state interventionism remained, however, influential, and politicians relied on the mechanics of deficit-spending. The economic sins
of the 1970s showed their negative effects above all in the 1980s. It is ironic that
with hindsight the 1980s are regarded as a period of relatively great economic
stability. A growing GDP seemed to reduce the importance of public debt totals,
especially when their size measured as percentage of GDP remained fairly constant,
though this did not mean that in every country studied here this percentage was
automatically low. The world economy of the 1980s was not only writing this –
as it was perceived – economic success story by its own dynamic. An important
contribution to economic fortunes was made by the deficit spending of the United
States in order to finance President Reagan's ambitious military programmes. Federal borrowing to finance that kind of public expenditure also had the effect of high
interest rates in the United States. This was the Federal Reserve's firewall against
inflation. High interest rates operated as a strong incentive for non-US investors to
bring their capital to the United States. This in turn was an important source for the
capital the US Government needed to borrow.

What are the limits of public borrowing? This question has been addressed from
different perspectives. Many economists have assumed a negative impact of the
public debt on the economic performance of national economies. To find direct and
causal links is, however, not as easy as common sense might suggest. Both Britain
and the United States have been enjoying economic success for a couple of years,
although their respective public debt totals have not been reduced. If we take two
important indicators for economic success, low interest rates and price stability, we
find no significant correlation to public borrowing.

Another argument of economists in this context is that the shrinking room for
manoeuvre for policy initiatives caused by deficits will eventually lead to a breakdown of public budgeting. Interest payments have already become one of the major
budget items in all four countries. Additional annual deficits and eventually an

upward trend of the interest rate level as we progress on the rate cycle will raise rate costs in the future. When (or if) the whole budget is needed to service capital costs, this is definitely the end of public borrowing. The question we asked – what are the limits of public borrowing – is difficult to answer, because the answer to this question lies somewhere in between the short-term impression that borrowing and economic success are compatible and the long-term prospect of nations losing altogether their ability to control their budgets.

The most accepted yardstick to measure public debt is the debt-to-GDP ratio. There is, however, a problem for politicians who rely on this indicator. The size of the GDP is much more elastic than the level of debts. It can shrink or stagnate as well as grow, whereas the fact that interests have to be paid on public debt means that as long as no serious effort is made to repay public debt it will keep growing no matter what a country's economic performance is like. The last few decades have confronted us with instances of economic recession and simultaneously comparatively high debt levels. One important consequence has been that the share of spending necessary to serve the public debt has grown to such an extent that the ability of governments to do more than preside over the administration of existing legislation has been seriously impaired.

The easy way out of this dilemma seems to be privatisation, but this is for obvious reasons a very limited strategic choice. Once all publicly owned estates and companies are sold this source of government income dries up. For Britain, North Sea oil worked in the Thatcher years to some extent as a *deus ex machina* which helped the government to reduce both annual deficits and Britain's overall indebtedness. One pre-condition for such a success story is, however, relatively high world market prices for oil. And even then oil income is not necessarily helping national governments to balance their budgets. In Canada it became clear that the western provinces were not willing to finance the federal government with what they regarded as benefits from their own resources.

In countries in which no special circumstances offered some relief from the deficit problem, the logical consequence could only be either to reduce spending or to increase taxes. The first strategy was facilitated by a paradigm change in the economic advice decision-makers received. Keynesianism had in the 1970s slowly lost its influence. The idea that in times of economic boom governments would reduce their spending and raise taxes to repay their debts proved unworkable in practice. This did not prevent, however, higher taxes for other purposes. The re-election incentive which tells politicians to keep on spending to win over voters was always stronger than a politician's ambition to be faithful to some abstract economic doctrine, such as Keynesianism, which no ordinary voter understands.

The alternative for deficit control, an increase in public income, for example through higher taxes, was, however, recently more or less ruled out, at least with regard to direct taxes – the taxation of companies and of individuals – because of the international competition of tax regimes which started in the 1980s. The aim of this competition was and still is first to attract foreign direct investment and, secondly, to prevent the loss of domestic investment to foreign countries in order to stimulate and maintain national economic growth. Though the hope of some politicians, above all of President Reagan, that lower taxes would in this way lead to an increased tax income, was nowhere translated into reality, no government could afford to drive investors out of the country by tax increases which further widened the gap between high- and low-tax countries.

Party politics did not matter much in respect to such policies. We have seen that Keynesianism as an economic strategy was based on just as broad a party political coalition as is the present economic strategy, which is based upon the optimistic belief in the ability of markets to optimise economic success. It is true that conservative governments in all countries were the first ones to deal seriously with the deficit problem, but not always very vigorously. The German Conservative Government is still muddling through and not until well into Kohl's second term was priority given to anti-deficit policies. The anti-deficit mood of the Reagan administration was surprisingly selective. The defence budget was deliberately excluded from efforts to control spending. David Stockman, President Reagan's first budget director, cites the President who said, 'Defense . . . is not a budget issue. You spend what you need' (Stockman 1986: 303). In Germany a Conservative Government initiated the greatest ever debt explosion in the history of the Federal Republic when it decided to finance German unification mostly by money borrowed on the capital markets. The mostly bipartisan approach to the deficit problem is easy to prove in the cases where Conservative Governments had successors who were regarded as traditionally to the left of them. After coming to power neither Bill Clinton in the United States, nor Jean Chrétien in Canada nor Tony Blair in Britain have indicated that they wanted to turn the clock back in budgetary politics, i.e. that they favoured the recipes of Keynesianism.

Ronald Reagan and Margaret Thatcher have, because of their strong positions as heads of government and their personalities, certainly helped to bury Keynesianism as a doctrine and have therefore delegitimised deficits as an economic instrument. Still, even in the post-Keynesian era, special circumstances have been used to justify additional deficits.

The four-country comparison shows that Westminster systems of government are best suited to break with past spending habits. Much depends, of course, on the strength of convictions a government with a new approach holds and its political strength. Margaret Thatcher's weaker position in Cabinet in her earlier years in government forced her to be more careful with regard to spending reductions than she was later. Although her successor, John Major, in theory supported the idea of a balanced budget, both economic circumstances and his style of government prevented him from making full use of the instruments of deficit control the Westminster system provides. In the highly politicised environment of budgetary policy-making legal instruments for budget control are fairly rare. Where they exist they are often themselves transformed into a weapon in the arsenal of party political competition. This is true both for the efforts to introduce balanced budget amendments to constitutions on the national and subnational level, for example in the United States, and for more flexible ways to limit annual deficits, such as the provision in the German constitution that with the exception of extraordinary economic circumstances deficits should not exceed the level of planned investments.

However, as was reported recently, a new consensus seems to have emerged in the United States. Workable, even though less than perfect, institutional reforms and, most importantly, a good economic performance led to a balanced budget in the United States before the year 2000. Unlike Germany, Canada and Britain, which each have only 'executive budgets', the United States has two competing budget proposals, the Presidential and the Congressional one. The traditional assumption was that pork-barrel spending and institutionalised gridlock between committees and government branches stall progress towards the aim of balancing the budget. But today, significant progress has become undeniable. Political scientists are now confronted with the surprising new question: what accounts for this 'policy success'?

A comparison of federal and non-federal countries in our sample shows that federal countries tend to rediscover subnational governments in times of financial crisis both as convenient players which can be burdened with costly tasks central governments want to get rid of and/or as a level of government for which, from the central governments' point of view, expenditures should or may be cut. This can be done more easily in the United States, with a relatively clear separation of responsibilities, or in Canada, with a relatively limited number of joint federal–provincial responsibilities. It is more complicated and has been less successful in the German case (Sturm 1997). If we look at general public debt totals most efforts of federal governments to shift financial burdens to lower-level governments remained unsuccessful, because national debt totals include the debt of subnational governments.

An important institutional factor for the size of the public deficit are the rules of the decision-making process on the budget. They include the relative strength of the executive and parliament and the veto power the constitution gives certain political actors. Bargaining may affect different levels of government, but it is also present in the relationship between US Congress and the President or inside governments between coalition partners and/or the guardians of the budget (most of the time the Finance Ministers) and the spending ministers. The veto of the Finance Minister or the veto of the President has serious consequences for the course the deficit takes.

There is no doubt that budgetary institutions matter when it comes to deficit control policies, but reality seems to be too complex to be reduced to monocausality. So far, qualitative comparative research has produced more insights than methods which rely on 'number-crunching'. Such comparative approaches which try to correlate statistically a number of factors with the size of deficits come to broad conclusions which common sense would suggest to every citizen anyhow, for example, that, 'Both the performance of the economy and of the political system appear to be contributing factors in producing a deficit' (Peters 1991: 126).

With the growing number of off-budget budgets and other clever devices of 'creative budgeting' it has become increasingly difficult to identify how big budget deficits are. Even more complicated is the answer to the question, how 'bad' they are. Public perceptions of the deficit vary over time, and those affected by the financial consequences of deficits were in most cases neither involved in the relevant decisions or too young or not even around when they were taken. There is also a time lag between debates on the deficit and actions taken. In the United

States, deficit control became an issue in its own right in the 1980s when for the first time in American history serious efforts were made to stop the growth of deficits by federal legislation. The deficit became a central topic of domestic politics, because other policies, especially social policies, were now made dependent on the success of greater financial discipline. Margaret Thatcher took similar decisions in Britain at about the same time, though motivated less by the feeling that her country lacked the resources for additional expenditures, than by the monetarist belief in the need for a better control of the money supply to the economy in order to control inflation. In both countries deficit control policies were also strongly connected with the idea that cutting expenditures would be a successful strategy for reducing the role of the state in the economy. Big government was seen as a source of economic ills, and the deficit as an expression of this phenomenon.

In Germany and Canada serious efforts to control the deficit did not start until the late 1980s and early 1990s. Though in the public debate of both countries attention for the issue was raised already in the early 1980s (during the 1980 election campaign in Germany and in the first years of Brian Mulroney's Government), governments in Canada and Germany found it difficult to challenge the welfare state to the degree which was implied by policies of expenditure control. In the meantime the alarming growth rate of the deficit in Canada which has resulted in an increase of the net public debt total of Canadian federal and provincial governments from 74.7 per cent of GDP in 1989–90 to 105.9 per cent of GDP in 1996–7 forced Canadian governments on all political levels to react, even if this meant introducing extremely unpopular cut-back policies. In Germany not only the deficit, but also budgeting itself got out of control as a result of a combination of at least two factors. First, the efforts of German industry to increase its competitiveness, and the structural weakness of Germany's economy, led to massive job losses. These social costs of industrial change greatly accelerated the growth of the deficit. Second, German unification, mostly deficit-financed, contributed directly to the growing debt level. In Germany (as in the United States for other reasons) budget planning is often difficult for the executive and the whole budgetary process has become unpredictable. Hitherto unusual techniques, such as supplementary budgets or the provision that after the budget has been passed every single item of expenditure of spending ministries above a certain amount still needs the special consent of the finance minister (*Haushaltssperre*), have become routine instruments to deal with unexpected deficits.

Who are the whistle-blowers who bring the deficit problem to public attention? As mentioned above, over time the problem of public deficits became somewhat self-evident. But still, different groups of people and interests have promoted public awareness. In Germany the *Bundesbank* and the Council of Economic Advisors (*Sachverständigenrat*) have long been playing the role of a watch-dog. In the United States think tanks and fiscal conservatives have fulfilled this function. In Britain higher public awareness of the deficit problem appears to be mainly due to an ideological shift initiated by the newly elected governments of the 1980s, whereas for Canada the pressure of international money markets and the close relationship of the country's economy with the US economy is decisive.

In all countries the greatest worry of politicians must be that a growing total indebtedness, and especially the annual payments which have to be made to service the debt, reduce their ability to govern. If a first large part of the budget has to be used to pay interests on the national debt, if a second large part of the budget is reserved for minimal efforts to secure peace (defence and law and order), and if a third large part of the budget is inflexible, because it finances spending obligations to which citizens are legally entitled, what room for manoeuvre remains for new policy initiatives? Aaron Wildavsky (1988) has aptly summarised this dilemma for politicians by his question: 'If you can't budget, how can you govern?' Strategic changes which may alleviate the pressure of public deficits are mostly long-term in their effects whereas the expectations of voters and electoral cycles which structure decision-making are short term. This means, in other words, that politicians not only lack the room for manoeuvre for new policy initiatives but they are also often unable to create the room for manoueuvre for deficit control policies which are the precondition for a gradual increase in their ability to regain control over the deficit problem, rather than merely reacting to the dynamics of public indebtedness.

Deficit control politics vary with regard to the degree to which they are formalised. In Canada and Britain a change in the consensus on the direction of budgeting, on spending priorities and on the containment of taxation, has contributed a great deal to budgetary discipline. In addition, different systems of expenditure control on the Cabinet level have been tried out. It turned out that in the world of politics and especially public spending there is no such thing as a 'neutral' opinion of a minister. Devices to create ministerial committees which control spending ministers or the idea that ministers share a budget total and allocate spending 'rationally', i.e. only with regard to what is most efficient and in the interest of the common good, have all been unsuccessful. Even in times of economic boom periods with budget surpluses the distribution of public goods is not easy and will define winners and losers. It is even more difficult in times of economic crisis and of deficits when deficit control policies produce only losers and no winners at all. The relevant question for a minister then is, how can I limit my losses? Ministerial committees to distribute losses are also superfluous, because across-the-board cuts could well be decreed centrally. Ministerial committees, on the other hand, with the task of making meaningful choices, will not decide on the relative merit of programme proposals – their decisions will be made as the result of internal power struggles. Prime Ministers know this very well. In the Canadian case the Prime Minister as the source of power on the Cabinet level has been the more successful in his efforts to control expenditures the more he centralised decision-making, for example by introducing a system of guardians of public expenditures to make sure that once decisions are made they are also implemented. In the British case in addition to Prime Ministerial strength there is always the possibility of strengthening the Treasury to control expenditures. Deficit control by the Treasury can be formalised by internal Treasury procedures which allow the Treasury to put forward 'neutral' arguments for the kind of allocation of funds it prefers.

In Germany and the United States more formal arrangements to control the deficit have been put in place. Although the advocates of this idea in the United

States have repeatedly tried, a constitutional amendment which would prescribe a balanced budget on the federal level has not been passed. Nevertheless, balanced budgets have become the guideline for American states and Canadian provinces. Balanced budget amendments are not only a budgetary matter. They also imply a deep distrust of politicians and the assumption that only a legal barrier which majority voting in Congress cannot easily remove will stop politicians from over-spending. This does not mean that politicians would automatically complain about such a limitation of their freedom of decision-making in budgeting. For them it may be convenient to get rid of some of their responsibility in these matters. In some cases it may even be the only chance for politicians to escape the pressure of interest groups with their own spending priorities.

What else is the search for institutional solutions to the deficit problem than an acknowledgement that political decision-making processes suffer from major insti-tutional deficiencies? When it comes to political reforms the question is whether to cure symptoms, i.e. change budgetary rules, or to tackle ultimate causes, i.e. the suboptimal system of constitutional governance. Constitutional reform has, how-ever, made little progress so far. The balanced budget constitutional amendment on the federal level, which has not found the necessary political majorities in the United States, would, for obvious reasons, be no solution for Britain, one of the few states in the world without a written constitution. A constitutional ban on deficits could potentially be a solution for Germany. There have been cautious efforts to initiate a debate on this idea – at least on the subnational level. But no other country has so persistently favoured this specific approach of deficit control as the United States. The sheer size of the public debt in the United States may explain to some extent why this is the case.

A second-best solution to constitutional limits to deficits are those decreed by legislation. The typical example for such a piece of legislation is the Gramm–Rudman–Hollings Act discussed above. As has been pointed out, the basic problem with legislation to control deficits is that majorities in the legislature can also legislate to increase the flexibility of their own legislation. Especially in a context of continuous bargaining, which is typical for the US Congress, a bargained excep-tion to deficit rules or the stretching of the rules is always more likely than the strict discipline implied by budget control legislation. Still, one should not underestimate the psychological and political pressures originating from efforts of Congress to bind itself. The general consensus behind such decisions was at least strong enough to keep the topic of deficit control at the top of the political agenda for more than a decade now, and Congress has refined its legislation to a point at which it now seems to be more likely that deficit control policies have enough teeth to bite.

As described above, Germany has constitutional rules for the size of an accept-able deficit, but these rules have more holes than a Swiss cheese. In the German case the government can play around with the definition of investments whose size limits the size of the deficit. And if everything goes wrong, as for example with the 1997 budget, there is the easy way out to mobilise the government majority in Parliament which will then conclude that Germany's economy is in serious imbalance (in 1997 because of high unemployment rates). In such exceptional circumstances the German constitution allows additional spending. The idea behind this kind of deficit spending was once to stimulate the economy according to the logic of Keynesian demand management. In 1996, a Conservative Government, which long ago had declared that the years of Keynesianism were over, was happy to use this provision in the constitution as an escape clause to legalise its overspending. The German example demonstrates in an extreme way that there are very definite limits to an institutional control of the deficit. Budgetary politics cannot be substituted for some ingenious mechanism which automatically controls deficits. The efficiency and effectiveness of institutional arrangements depends critically on the political consensus in a society, on a deficit control concept developed by decision-makers and social coalitions which support deficit control policies.

To forge such coalitions is not easy. In all countries looked at in this book it is clear that whereas capital owners may profit to some extent from high interest rates or the offers governments have to make to finance their deficits by recourse to the capital markets, for the greater part of society deficit control policies remain abstract in their value. Those who are more or less dependent on state infrastructure, government jobs and social transfers are affected negatively by deficit control policies. Direct taxes have rarely been raised to create additional income for the state. If taxes are increased at all, mostly indirect taxes are affected. Taxes on consumption hit low-income earners harder than high-income earners. Higher taxes on consumption together with lower social expenditures have made deficit control policies widely unpopular. Seen in context such policies have contributed to the opening of the gap between the rich and the poor in all four societies studied here.

In general, the social consequences of deficit control policies are, however, far from clear. Budgetary policy always mirrors the whole range of government policies for they all have financial consequences. Thus deficit control policies can hardly be 'neutral' with regard to their effects on other policies. Spending on social policies is a major budget item in all four countries studied here, so it is hardly surprising that deficit control efforts aim at reforming social policies. There is apparently a broad consensus that public spending cannot continue to be what it has been for the last three decades or so. The policy choice is difficult. Decision-makers can either close their eyes on the new realities and muddle through without a concept of reform. This means, however, that the problems of governability will very soon dominate not only the agenda of social policies, but also of policy-making in general. Or they can decide to reform social policies in order to rescue some of the most important features of the welfare state. Which features these may be depends, of course, on what kind of future relationship between state and society politicians and citizens see as appropriate. It is unlikely, however, that the decisions about core spending programmes will only be made on a theoretical level. Social reform will have to respect the political pressure of organised interests and their ability to form broader political coalitions in societies.

Deficit control policies have not only a national but also an international dimension both with regard to their origins and with regard to their consequences. The treaty of Maastricht and the European Monetary Union (EMU) have exerted strong pressure on the EU member states to rearrange their budgets by the year 1998 at the latest in order to meet the deficit criteria as laid down in a protocol to the Maastricht treaty. Britain's opt-out of the Monetary Union has given the country more breathing space and the chance to decide at a later stage whether Britain wants to be part of EMU or not. Still, John Major's Chancellor of the Exchequer, Kenneth Clarke, wrote his budget proposals with Maastricht in mind. However, among the countries studied here it was above all Germany for which the Maastricht criteria set limits to its annual budget deficit and to its total indebtedness. These limits set by an international treaty had to be taken much more seriously than the country's constitutional provisions. The Maastricht criteria had the effect not only of raising public awareness of the debt problem, they also contributed considerably to the legitimacy and the urgency of deficit control policies. Economists may debate whether the exact numbers the Maastricht criteria refer to as guidelines (budget deficit not more than 3 per cent of GDP, total debt not more than 60 per cent of GDP) make economic sense or not. The new insight the Maastricht experiment has given us is that international obligations may be able to play an important role with regard to the control of national deficits, if what is internationally at stake (here the future of European integration) is important enough to the government and elites (here especially German export industries) of a certain society.

The lack of deficit control regularly mobilises the central banks when they fear that the additional demand for credit created by deficits will produce inflation. One consequence of central bank intervention may be high interest rates which encourage foreign capital owners to transfer their capital to such a high-interest country. This move of capital to high-interest countries urges other economies to adjust their levels of interest rates upward in order to provide for a competitive environment for capital investments. Thus, if one country's budgetary policy leads to higher interest rates, this will soon result in a higher level of capital cost elsewhere. One could argue that by such a 'tax' on the world President Reagan's Star Wars programme as well as German unification were co-financed.

Critics (Peters 1991: 130) have pointed out that the consequences of an 'internationalisation' of a country's debt problem may lead to three problems: (a) the debtor nation becomes dependent upon its creditors and to some degree must tailor its policies to ensure a stable environment for borrowing, (b) the national economy becomes vulnerable to rapid movements of capital out of the country and (c) interest must be paid abroad, i.e. rather than just causing an internal transfer of funds the servicing of the national debt becomes a net loss to the economy. These critics overestimate the power of creditors. None of the four countries of our analysis seems to be in the stranglehold of its creditors. Foreign investment in government bonds has not yet reached a level which creates the danger of giving creditors from abroad a say in government policies. No matter how important globalisation may be, states are still sovereign and thus remain ultimately responsible for their budgets and their respective currency. A second point to be noted is that interest payments to foreign investors do not mean a net loss of resources. Economically speaking, interests are prices for the use of capital. In the world of private business, foreign investment which leads to future interest payments and the repayment of debts to foreign capital owners, is not only regarded as unproblematic, it is often the rule. Therefore the important question is for which purpose borrowed money is used and what kinds of usage are crowded out. It did not matter much in the past whether capital came from domestic or foreign investors – and it does not matter today in a world with globalised financial markets.

After so much gloom and criticism evoked by the deficit problem one should be allowed to ask the question Erich Kästner, a famous twentieth-century German author, was once asked: 'Herr Kästner, wo bleibt das Positive?' (Mr Kästner, when will you start saying something positive?). Some consolation can be found in the analysis of scientists who prefer a long-term perspective. Harold Chorney (1996: 375) takes such an optimistic view when he writes:

> Over time, it is likely that adjustments will be made that restore the relationship
> between recovery, higher growth rates and job creation. Once this occurs, the flow of
> revenues to government will increase enormously and, coupled with the higher growth
> rate, the debt and deficit problem will fade away.

But even if Chorney is not right, one could ask the modest question: what is positive about public debts? One could argue that deficits have, in a twisted way, also improved things. They have reintroduced economic categories into government policies. In the era of Keynesianism raising money seemed to be a relatively unimportant problem. Politics could concentrate on expenditures, especially on the development of a system of transfers and subsidies. The debate on the public debt has not only reminded all of us that it is difficult to spend more than you earn, it also forces us – and this is of greater and further-reaching importance – to think differently about budgets. Deficits are no longer just what remains when all the important decisions are taken. The important decisions to be taken now include the ones concerning the deficit. This implies the idea that spending and taxation have to be looked at simultaneously and no longer separately and sequentially as formerly. The unity of the budget is also synonymous at least with regard to its financial aspects as to what a government does or plans to do. Governance which is deficit-driven rather than policy-driven may eventually get into major problems of legitimacy. If resources can no longer be allocated by political initiatives, politics loses one of its basic sources of legitimacy.

Fundamental reforms of the relationship between the state and the economy and between the state and the society may therefore be one result of the pressures exerted by deficits. Politicians have said they would never have touched such a sensitive issue had it not been for the financial plight their country was in. One should, of course, not exaggerate this point. Political reform, at least in theory, does not need a doomsday scenario to get started. The debt crisis is only special in one way. It will not go away when it is ignored.

References

Chorney, Harold (1996) 'Debits, deficits and full employment', in: Boyer, Robert and Drache, Daniel (eds), *States Against Markets. The Limits of Globalization*, London and New York: Routledge.

Peters, Guy (1991) *The Politics of Taxation. A Comparative Perspective*, Oxford: Blackwell.

Stockman, David (1986) *The Triumph of Politics. The Crisis in American Government and How it Affects the World*, London: Bodley Head.

Sturm, Roland (1997) 'Föderalismus in Deutschland und den USA – Tendenzen der Angleichung?', in: *Zeitschrift für Parlamentsfragen* 28(2), pp. 335–45.

Wildavsky, Aaron (1988) 'If you can't budget, how can you govern?', in: Anderson, Annelise and Bark, Dennis L. (eds), *Thinking About America. The United States in the 1990s*, Stanford: Stanford UP, pp. 266–75.

Index